CLASSIC S
ON REVIVAL AND
SPIRITUAL RENEWAL

KREGEL CLASSIC SERMONS Series

KREGEL CLASSIC | SERMONS SERIES

CLASSIC SERMONS ON REVIVAL AND SPIRITUAL RENEWAL

Compiled by
Warren W. Wiersbe

kregel
PUBLICATIONS

Grand Rapids, MI 49501

Classic Sermons on Revival and Spiritual Renewal,
compiled by Warren W. Wiersbe

Published by Kregel Publications, a division of Kregel,
Inc., P.O. Box 2607, Grand Rapids, MI 49501. Kregel Publications provides trusted, biblical publications for Christian
growth and service. Your comments and suggestions are
valued.

Cover photo: Art Jacobs
Cover and Book Design: Alan G. Hartman

Library of Congress Cataloging-in-Publication Data

Classic sermons on revival and spiritual renewal /
compiled by Warren W. Wiersbe.
     p.   cm.— (Kregel classic sermons series)
    Includes index.
    1. Church renewal—Sermons. 2. Evangelistic work—
Sermons. 3. Sermons, English. 4. Sermons, American.
I. Wiersbe, Warren W. II. Series: Kregel classic sermons
series.
BV3797.A1C57   1995   269—dc20   95-37069
                                             CIP

ISBN   0-8254-4062-9 (pbk.)

      1 2 3 4 5 Printing / Year 99 98 97 96 95

Printed in the United States of America

CONTENTS

LIST OF SCRIPTURE TEXTS

PREFACE

THE *KREGEL CLASSIC SERMONS SERIES* is an attempt to assemble and publish meaningful sermons from master preachers about significant themes.

These are *sermons*, not essays or chapters taken from books about themes. Not all of these sermons could be called "great," but all of them are *meaningful*. They apply the truths of the Bible to the needs of the human heart, which is something that all effective preaching must do.

While some are better known than others, all of the preachers whose sermons I have selected had important ministries and were highly respected in their day. The fact that a sermon is included in this volume does not mean that either the compiler or the publisher agrees with or endorses everything that the man did, preached, or wrote. The sermon is here because it has a valued contribution to make.

These are sermons about *significant* themes. The pulpit is no place to play with trivia. The preacher has thirty minutes in which to help mend broken hearts, change defeated lives, and save lost souls; and he can never accomplish this demanding ministry by distributing homiletical tidbits. In these difficult days we do not need "clever" pulpiteers who discuss the times; we need dedicated ambassadors who will preach the eternities.

The reading of these sermons can enrich your spiritual life. The studying of them can enrich your skills as an interpreter and expounder of God's truth. However God uses these sermons in your life and ministry, my prayer is that His Church around the world will be encouraged and strengthened by them.

WARREN W. WIERSBE

What the Spirit Is Saying to the Churches

James S. Stewart (1896–1990) pastored three churches in Scotland before becoming professor of theology at the University of Edinburgh (1936) and then professor of New Testament (1946). But he was a professor who preached, a scholar who applied biblical truth to the needs of common people, and a theologian who made doctrine practical and exciting. He published several books of lectures and biblical studies including *A Man in Christ* and *Heralds of God*. His two finest books of sermons are *The Gates of New Life* and *The Strong Name*.

This sermon is taken from *The Wind of the Spirit*, published in 1968 by Abingdon Press, Nashville. Used by permission.

James S. Stewart

1

WHAT THE SPIRIT IS SAYING TO THE CHURCHES

He that hath an ear, let him hear what the Spirit saith unto the churches (Revelation 2:7).

THE SPIRIT IS assuredly saying some radical things to the churches today. There is a stirring in the life of all the churches which means that God the Holy Spirit is speaking. Through the tumult and the shouting of international controversy, through the clash and the clang of modern materialist civilization, through the tangled complexity of ecclesiastical debate, through the problems and bewilderments of our own hearts, a deeper note keeps beating—the Spirit of God crying to those who have ears to hear.

John wrote to seven churches in Asia, not because there were only seven (for actually there were far more), not because these seven lay geographically in a circle, but because seven is symbolical—it is the perfect number—so that in writing to these seven he writes to all, to the Church Universal, to all congregations of Christian people scattered everywhere throughout the world: to Britain and America, to Germany and Africa and India. We ourselves are part of this. He writes to you and me.

Now each of the letters has one distinctive note, a single operative word or vital challenging phrase to sum up the whole message. I suggest that we should listen to these different notes for they will give us what the Holy Spirit is saying to the churches now.

The Church at Ephesus

Here, to begin with, is Ephesus. What does the Spirit say to the church at Ephesus? The Spirit says—*Repent.* "Thou hast left thy first love: remember, therefore, and repent."

9

Now think of the church anywhere—Ephesus, Geneva, Canterbury, Edinburgh, New York. We are the church of four mighty historical acts: the Church of the Incarnation, of the Cross, of the Resurrection, of Pentecost. Can we measure up to any of these descriptions of the church without penitence and contrition?

The Church of the Incarnation, of the Word who was made flesh, who never stood aloof in a superior holiness, but gladly came right down for love of men into the fearful pit and the miry clay and the multiple miseries of all mankind; right into a world that had things in it as frightful as Belsen and Buchenwald and Hiroshima. All the outcasts felt at home with Him, and He called the harlots friends. We are hardly like that, are we, with our too often disincarnate pieties, our disembodied theologies, our ecclesiastical self-segregation, our rationalizing busyness designed precisely to avoid the embarrassment of giving ourselves away? Church of the Incarnation, says the Holy Spirit, remember and repent!

The Church of the Cross, and not, mark you, the cross of the stained-glass window and the silver ornament, not the cross about which it is all too easy to wax eloquent or even sentimental. But the cross which for Jesus meant total abnegation, stark and painful, total reversal of the world's whole scale of values, self just blotted out. We are not like that normally, who so easily become infected in the church by secular ideas of what constitutes prosperity and success and importance and security. Church of the Cross, says the Spirit, remember and repent!

The Church of the Resurrection, that is to say, the church of the greatest, gladdest, best of news that ever startled men's ears and shattered the midnight of their souls. The church that once went singing through the world and shouting through the martyr fires, "He is risen. Hallelujah—Christ is risen!" We are not like that, are we, who contrive to take our holy faith so dreadfully sedately, submerged in our dull tedious routine? Church of the Resurrection, remember and repent!

The Church of Pentecost, where men heard the rushing mighty wind and saw the descending fire; where they spoke in new tongues of the wonderful works of God; where they were all with one accord in one place, welded into the most vital unity of fellowship the world has ever seen. We are not like that, are we? We feel ashamed sometimes at our supineness and shocked at our divisions: and I mean shocked not merely at their waste and stupidity, but shocked at their sinfulness. For the Lord God is calling us to go out and preach reconciliation to the nations, to society, to all the broken lives of men. How can we preach it when we are notoriously divided ourselves? Certainly the difficulties are real and formidable, admitting of no facile solution. But the fact remains that there are doctrines we hold in common, and facts which these doctrines enshrine, so incomparably miraculous, so world-shattering in their significance, so humanly speaking incredible, that they dwarf everything that keeps us apart. If we really believe the great facts of our faith—incarnation, atonement, resurrection—not vaguely assenting to them as articles in a creed but truly imagining them and seeing them, held and possessed by them, must they not outweigh everything else, and must not their uniting power be stronger than the centrifugal forces that rend the church asunder? Can we go on indefinitely debating secondary things, with Christ standing there declaring, "Before Abraham was, I am"? It appears that we can. This is the catastrophic stubbornness of human sin. And it just will not do to pride ourselves that we at least do not create the problem, that all the barriers are on the other side of some ecclesiastical fence; for that is to thank God that we are not as other men and churches are and is there not a parable of Jesus to say that that is precisely the sin that can most effectively damn the soul? Church of Pentecost, remember and repent!

This is the word for the Church in Ephesus: Repent. And he that has an ear, let him hear what the Spirit is saying to the churches.

The Church at Smyrna

Here is Smyrna. What does the Spirit say to the church

at Smyrna? The Spirit says—*Realize your riches.* "I know your poverty, but you are rich."

Now this might be called the very signature tune of the New Testament. The New Testament is not a dull treatise on ethical theism or mild humanitarianism or respectable behavior. It is much more like a wild treasure island story, throbbing with the exhilaration of stupendous discovery, fabulous wealth, colossal unsearchable riches. And mark you, this is not fairy-tale and make-believe. That God bears the sins of the world, this—even in a world of electronic brains and artificial satellites and technical marvels of all kinds—is the ultimate mystery and the irrefragable truth. That Christ communicates life—this is the redeeming of existence from meaninglessness and insignificance. For the moment you can say, "I live, yet not I, but Christ liveth in me," you are into a new dimension. Your human nature has been laid hold of by super-nature. To use our Lord's own figure, just as the vine injects its life into the branch, so Christ imparts to His church and to all who will receive Him the very life of God: not just an improved existence, but actually God's own quality of life.

The trouble is that we will not believe it. Hence you get the appalling difference between the magnificent audacity of the church's creed and the dull conventionality of its life. It is because we do not fully believe it that we are all at sixes and sevens. And so when Julian Huxley at the University of Chicago's Darwinian centenary celebrations prophesied the emergence of a new religion without revelation or the supernatural, or Earl Russell tells us, "Why I am not a Christian," when one school of psychology sponsors "morals without religion" and another expounds conversion in terms of brainwashing, there are Christians who start trembling for the ark of God. It is so absurdly unnecessary. For as "heirs of God, joint-heirs with Christ," we hold the title-deeds of our inheritance here and now, life eternal in the midst of time, the first anticipatory sample and installment of the heavenly kingdom: so that all the arguments of all the Huxleys and Russells and death-of-God theologians are impotent and ineffective and ultimately irrelevant.

Come, Almighty to deliver,
Let us all Thy life receive.

This is the word for the church in Smyrna: Realize
your riches. And he that has an ear, let him hear what
the Spirit is saying to the churches.

The Church at Pergamos

Here is Pergamos. What does the Spirit say to the
church at Pergamos? The Spirit says—*Stand for freedom!*
He says, "Resist the encroaching pressure of power politics and pagan ideologies." For this is the meaning of the
cryptic double reference to "Satan's throne." "You have to
live your life," he tells them twice over, "where Satan sits
enthroned." This is an oblique reference to the Caesar
worship of the imperial cult at Pergamos, in which a mili-
tant totalitarian political secularism loomed with a bale-
ful hatred upon the men and women who were Christ's
church. Stand for freedom!

Ancient history? It is nothing of the kind. I think of our
fellow Christians in China, with the perpetual problem
confronting them. "How far can we go with the present
government, and where have we to stop and refuse to
collaborate, saying 'Here stand I; I can do no other; so
help me God'?" I think of our fellow Christians in certain
parts of Africa, some of them dictated to by a totalitarian
law which says, "You may worship in this church but not
in that"—as though the church could be ordered about by
a department of state and were not the house of the living
God, the pillar and ground of the truth. I think of the
pressures there are in present-day society to get people,
young people especially, to consent to and acquiesce in
sub-Christian standards of culture: "Conform, or be left
out!"—which is secularism's dreary reversal of the ancient word, "Be not conformed to this world, but be transformed by the renewing of your mind." I think of one of
the greatest and most urgent of international problems,
the question of the proliferation of nuclear weapons and
the dangers of nuclear tests. Christians may take one
side or another quite sincerely. There are diversities of

judgment here. But at least we are bound to say this, that if any Christian, after deep, long searching of his soul and endeavoring to find the mind of Christ, should feel moved to speak out for abolition of such tests, and then encounters the contemptuous retort that he is a poor dupe, a misguided meddler, an unconscious victim of alien subtle propaganda—this at any rate is a libel and a lie. "Son of man, stand upon thy feet!"

This is the word for the church at Pergamos: Stand for freedom. And he that has an ear, let him hear what the Spirit is saying to the churches.

The Church at Thyatira

Here is Thyatira. What does the Spirit say to the church at Thyatira? The Spirit says—*Hold fast*. "That which ye have already hold fast till I come." This is Christian tenacity, that essential ingredient of discipleship. Hold out to the end!

Have you ever noticed, in reading the *Pilgrim's Progress*, how often Bunyan's pilgrim Christian, in journeying to the Celestial city, was met by pilgrims going the wrong way? For example, Timorous and Mistrust, who came running down the road shouting to him "Go back, man, go back! There are lions in the path!" Or like Mr. Pliable, who indeed made a splendid and encouraging beginning to the pilgrimage, outstripping the rest in his enthusiasm, until one day the Slough of Despond got hold of him, and he climbed out on the side nearest his own house, a pathetic, mud-bedraggled thing, and made tracks for home, and was never seen again?

That is the great danger—that you and I should lose heart in following Christ our King, and in the lengthening shadows should stand thinking back regretfully to the joy and confidence and dedication of earlier days now gone beyond recall, vanished in the devastating attrition of the years. When Paul wrote about Christians "starting in the Spirit and ending in the flesh"—which means, starting with devotion and ending with drudgery—he was referring to a risk from which none of us is immune.

Whither is fled the visionary gleam?
Where is it now, the glory and the dream?

It is pathetic; and the reason why it is so pathetic is precisely that it is utterly unnecessary. For this world has Pentecost in it. It is not a matter of summoning up our own resources. It is a matter of accepting God's gift. Why should we go on trying to live the Christian life in our own strength, when all the time God is offering us through the channels of prayer and dedication a resource and capacity of a totally different kind, new every morning, the identical power that made the men of Pentecost more than conquerors? This is the secret of serving Christ as long as life shall last with fresh, unwearied spirit. "They go from strength to strength; every one of them in Zion appeareth before God."

This is the word for the church at Thyatira: Hold fast. And he that has an ear, let him hear what the Spirit is saying to the churches.

The Church at Sardis

Here is Sardis. What does the Spirit say to the church at Sardis? The Spirit says—*Beware of nominal Christianity.* "Thou hast a name that thou livest"—you are nominally alive—"and art dead." You have all the paraphernalia of religion, the machinery, the organization; but the vital spark, the life, the creative, dynamic thing is not there.

That, at Sardis, was the tragedy. For as a rule what amazed and troubled and discomfited the Roman Empire about early Christianity was precisely its vitality. If they tried to put it down here, it would break out there. Wherever they touched it, they got something like an electric shock. "Look out," they began to say, "this new movement is dangerous. The thing's alive!"

But not here. Not at Sardis. "You have a name to live"—you are nominally Christian, but the luster has gone: the thing is not real!

Something must have happened in Sardis akin to what Albert Schweitzer said has been happening in our modern world. Look, said Schweitzer, at what the modern world has done to the great imperious demands of Jesus in the gospels. "Many of the greatest sayings are found lying in a corner like explosive shells from which the charges have been removed."

Paul told the Corinthians, "I may have this, and that, and the next thing, but if I have not love I am nothing." Similarly, what the Spirit is saying to the churches and telling some of us in the depths of our own hearts is this: I can have all the nominal Christianity in the world, but if I have not the life of Jesus I am nothing. I can intellectualize my religion, debating endlessly in discussion group the intricacies of creation and redemption, predestination and free will; I can legalize it, stressing the obligation of church attendance, Sabbath observance and so forth; I can institutionalize it, multiplying the apparatus of meetings and activities; I can standardize it, ritualize it, socialize it—but it is all worth precisely nothing, if I have not in me the life, the very life, of Jesus. "Nothing," wrote Kierkegaard, "is more dangerous to true Christianity than to get men to assume light-mindedly the name of Christian, as if it were something that one is as a matter of course." Hence we ought to be immensely grateful that in the Spirit poured out upon the church at Pentecost there is the divine antidote to all dull, competent, lusterless religion, the shattering of complacency and the end of being nominally Christian. "If ye know how to give good gifts to your children, how much more will your heavenly Father give the Holy Spirit to them that ask Him!"

This is the word for the church at Sardis: Beware of nominal Christianity. And he that has an ear, let him hear what the Spirit is saying to the churches.

The Church at Philadelphia

Here is Philadelphia. What does the Spirit say to the church at Philadelphia? The Spirit says—*Evangelize!* "Behold, I have set before thee an open door, and no man can shut it." Go out and evangelize! The very geographical position of Philadelphia gave this church a unique evangelizing opportunity. For Philadelphia stood at the head of the valley through which the great route from the western sea climbed to the hinterland of the central Asian plateau—the open door toward the cosmopolitan cities and commerce of the Orient. Philadelphia was the keeper of the gateway. And the Spirit says now to the church—That is your vocation: to go right out through that open gateway, not to sit down content in some cozy Christian circle of like-minded people, insulated against the swarming life of the great secular world, the bewilderments of the space-age, and the massive resurgence of non-Christian faiths; not to be

> a garden walled around,
> A little spot enclosed by grace
> Out of the world's wide wilderness,

but to be an expeditionary force, infiltrating the world of business and commerce and society in the name of Jesus. I have set before you an open door. Evangelize!

But what is modern evangelism? Mass meetings? Yes, certainly there is still a place for this. But surely something more. The House Church? The industrial mission? Vocational and visitation evangelism? All this indeed: but surely something more. Evangelism is a fellowship of reconciled and forgiven sinners feeling a personal responsibility and concern to make real to all men everywhere the reconciliation and forgiveness of God. Was it not William Temple who declared, "The church exists primarily for those who never go near it"? The real tragedy is when a church is not worried about those who never go near it, is quite content to leave the line of demarcation intact, looks askance at those out with its own spiritual like-minded family circle, maintains a mute, aloof, condemnatory apartheid from the secularism around its doors. In an introverted way that church may be flourishing, but it is certainly not Christian. What was the symbolism, asks the writer to the Hebrews, of Jesus' dying outside the gate, outside the camp, outside the walls of the holy city of Jerusalem? And he answers his own question. It is that we should now feel an irresistible constraint to "go forth to Him outside the camp, bearing His reproach." It is to burn it into our conscience that this is the surest place where Christ is to be found today, out in the world He died to redeem, and that to stay in the camp is to lose Him. Let me put it as bluntly as I can by saying this. Every time we raise a barrier of aloofness and condemnation between ourselves and the outside world, we are doing exactly what the man did in Jesus' parable who, having been pardoned by his master a frightful debt of a million pounds, could not forget that his neighbor owed him a wretched, paltry five-pound note. Jesus said that is the kind of righteousness that books a man for hell. This surely is evangelism, to have learned to say, "Who am I to condemn, when God has forgiven me so hugely?" This is evangelism: a reconciled, forgiven church not simply preaching, but living and offering to all men, the reconciliation and forgiveness of God.

This is the word for the church at Philadelphia: Evangelize. And he that has an ear, let him hear what the Spirit is saying to the churches.

The Church at Laodicea

Finally, here is Laodicea. What does the Spirit say to the church at Laodicea? The Spirit says—*Warm your faith at the fire of Jesus Christ.* Laodicea was told she was neither hot nor cold but simply tepid. It is not at all polite language here: I can't help that. "Because you are lukewarm, and neither cold nor hot, because your religion is tepid, you make Me sick!"

It is good that the risen Christ should employ such a devastating form of rebuke. For what chance has a tepid Christianity today? The opposition to Christianity is certainly not tepid. It is scorching.

Hence it is surely terribly foolish to suggest, as is sometimes done, that what is mainly needed for a renewal of the church is an overhaul of the machinery of church courts, or a democratization of church committees, or a resuscitation of the parochial system. All that may be necessary enough; but we need so much more—not a blueprint but a resurrection trumpet, not a few Acts of Assembly but the kindling contact of the flame of heaven. "Without enthusiasm," cried Joseph Parker once, "what is the church? It is Vesuvius without fire, it is Niagara without water, it is the firmament without the sun!'"

We know this is the church's need because we know it is our own. Each one of us would confess—"Lord, I have been such a poor specimen of what Your love can do, such a misleading advertisement of Your power." But we believe in the Holy Spirit. And we are here, all of us together, God's raw material for the building of His kingdom. And Christ still moves, as John saw Him, among the seven golden candlesticks or lampstands: He is still the One, the only One, who can make the churches shine or any cold heart catch fire.

This is the word for the church at Laodicea: Warm your faith at the fire of Jesus Christ. Or, turning it into a prayer, as each of us well might do: "O Light of all the world, relight my lamp today."

> Father, forgive the cold love of the years
> As here in the silence we bow;
> Perish our cowardice, perish our fears,
> Kindle us, kindle us now.
>
> Lord, we accept, we believe, we adore,
> Less than the least though we be;
> Fire of love, burn in us, burn evermore
> Till we burn out for Thee.

And he that has an ear, let him hear what the Spirit is saying to the churches.

The Conditions of Renewal

George Campbell Morgan (1863–1945) was the son of
a British Baptist preacher and preached his first sermon
when he was thirteen years old. He had no formal training
for the ministry, but his tireless devotion to the study of
the Bible helped him to become one of the leading Bible
teachers of his day. Rejected by the Methodists, he was
ordained into the Congregational ministry. He was
associated with Dwight L. Moody in the Northfield Bible
conferences and as an itinerant Bible teacher. He is best
known as the pastor of the Westminster Chapel, London
(1904–17 and 1933–45). During his second term there, he
had Dr. D. Martyn Lloyd-Jones as his associate.

Morgan published more than sixty books and booklets,
and his sermons are found in *The Westminster Pulpit*
(London, Hodder and Stoughton, 1906–1916). This sermon
is from Volume 8.

George Campbell Morgan

2

THE CONDITIONS OF RENEWAL

Repentance toward God, and faith toward our Lord Jesus Christ (Acts 20:21).

WE AT ONCE RECOGNIZE that this is not a sentence. As a matter of fact, the text consists of two phrases, incidentally employed in the course of apostolic discourse. Paul halted at Miletus in order that he might meet the elders of the church at Ephesus and speak to them, as he did not expect to see them again. In the course of his address delivered to those elders, in the interest of the church at Ephesus, and therefore as always in the interest of Ephesus itself, he reviewed the ministry which he had conducted in that city during three years; reminding them that he had not shrunk from declaring to them anything that was profitable, teaching them publicly and from house to house, testifying to both the Jews and the Greeks of "repentance toward God, and faith toward our Lord Jesus Christ."

In these phrases the apostle summarized the burden of his message in Ephesus in so far as that message emphasized personal and individual responsibility concerning the Gospel of the grace of God which he had proclaimed there. I have taken the words because they seem to me to give the simplest formula concerning human responsibility in the presence of the preaching of that Gospel of grace.

You will immediately see that the terms are those of spiritual things, spiritual relationships. It is quite easy, I think, to discover behind the words the apostolic outlook, the apostolic conception. It is quite evident that these phrases take for granted certain facts, while they reveal the immediate responsibility of men. There can be no meaning in them apart from certain facts which most

21

evidently were present in the mind of the apostle, facts, moreover, which he took for granted as being received and believed in by those to whom at this particular moment he was speaking.

What, then, are these underlying facts? First, the fact of God; second, the fact of man's relationship to God; third, the fact of man's being out of harmony with God; and, finally, the fact that a man out of harmony with God is a failure.

If we blot God out of our thinking or out of our belief, then there is no meaning in this text at all. It is only as we become conscious that the deep, true thing concerning ourselves is that we have relationship with God, that such relationship is at fault, and that therefore we are at fault, that there can be any appeal in such phrases as these.

Let us, then, proceed on the assumption that we take for granted the God of the Bible, the God from whom all things have proceeded, the God by whose power all things are upheld, from whose government nothing can ever by any possible chance escape.

Let us take for granted, in the second place, that man is spiritual, that the deepest, profoundest truth concerning man is that he is offspring of God, that the word which Ezekiel uttered long ago for the correction of false proverbs, "All souls are Mine," is a profound truth; that the deepest thing in each individual life is not the material, is not even the moral, but the spiritual; that, therefore, the things of change in the midst of which we find ourselves today cannot be the things which find us in the deepest of our lives; that, therefore, if we live only in relation to things seen and temporal, things that pass and vanish and perish even while we look on them, touch and handle them, we are ruining ourselves in that we are failing to realize the whole meaning of our lives.

Let us take for granted that we are children of the ages and not of the passing day, that we are in our essential being related to Deity and are not wholly of the dust; that to make the order of our life such as expresses itself, "Let us eat and drink, for tomorrow we die," is to fail entirely to understand ourselves. Let us further take for granted that if these things be so, then we are moving inevitably toward some change through which we shall come to a yet clearer apprehension of the reality of spiritual things and stand in the light of the Divine presence, in the nakedness of our spiritual life, stripped of all those things which today hide the spiritual from us, hide us so largely from each other, and hide us so perpetually from ourselves. If someone should say, Why do you not say plainly that we are all going to die? I would reply, Very well, let it be so stated—we are all approaching death! What is death? Death is but transition. Death is but the process of change by which personality passes from existence limited, hindered, probationary, into that which is larger, where the light is clearer, and the understanding perfected, and being comes to its fullness in some form or fashion. The reason for the fear of death is simply stated: "The sting of death is sin; and the power of sin is the law." Men do fear death, all their lifetime men are subject to bondage through the fear of death. The fear of death that rests on the heart of humanity is born of the fact that man is conscious that if he pass away from this life, with its limitations, into larger life, he is unprepared; he has not taken sufficient account of the larger life, has neglected the true aspiration of his nature, has not turned a listening ear to the voice forever sounding within him that he is immortal, eternal. Man lives within the narrow realm of the things that are near, and when he approaches the end, or things of the end, and imagines himself as passing out to some born whence no traveler returns, to some unknown state of being, he is filled with fear because of sin.

What, then, is sin? I pray you notice most carefully that this fear of death is not peculiar to men and women who have been guilty of what we sometimes term vulgar sins. Indeed, it is strange and yet true that the vulgar sensualist is often free from the fear of death, and because of that he has so completely blunted the spiritual in his sensuality that he has no consciousness of it whatever. The fear of death comes to finer souls—using the expression in the common language of our everyday speech.

What, then, is sin? Sin is failure. I use the word almost with bated breath, because to say that seems to rob sin of its terror. Yet consider it carefully. If the Bible, by the language of which it makes use, means anything, it conveys that idea. Confining ourselves for the moment to the New Testament, with which we are all familiar, the most common Greek word for sin, *hamartia*, means coming short, missing the mark. It is a Greek word which was used when a marksman shot an arrow at a target and failed to hit the center. Sin is failure. Sin is being less than I ought to be. Sin is failure to realize the meaning of my own life. Sin is failure to realize the forces that are within me. It is this sense of failure, this sense of limitation, this inner conviction that perchance never expresses itself in the language of a preacher, but, nevertheless, haunts the soul; this sense that the years are wasted, that the energies of life have not brought any true return to the personality—it is all this that overshadows man when he thinks of death. It is the true divine instinct within the soul telling it that when it sloughs off this mortal coil, and passes in the nakedness of its personality into the light of the uncreated beam, it will be seen crippled, dwarfed, atrophied, having failed to realize the profound meaning of life. That is the sense of sin.

There is in that sense of sin, moreover, the sense of pollution; or—use the word that helps you most—guilt, defilement, uncleanness. It is that sense that fills the heart with fear when death is spoken of.

For the sake of illustration, imagine a man who has no sense of failure, a man who has not failed, a man whose life has been clean, pure, straight, noble, and infinitely more than all these virtues, which mark conditions rather than realizations, a man who has found out the secret of his own being and has adjusted his life to its true center, who has filled his own vocation—that man never trembles at the thought of death. To him death is entrance on life. To him death is the hour in which, crossing the border line, he shall find himself in the presence of the uncreated beam. That is the goal of life, the high ecstasy toward which life is forever moving, the final moment when he will be able to stand unafraid in the presence of God and see the beatific vision, and find the last solution of all the problems of his own life as he rests in the presence of God. When such a man thinks of death, he says, "O death, where is thy victory? O death, where is thy sting? The sting of death is sin; and the power of sin is the law; but thanks be to God, which giveth us the victory through our Lord Jesus Christ."

In those final words of the apostolic challenge and affirmation I have introduced the Gospel of grace, and the real meaning of the Christian fact.

It is in the presence of such conceptions as these that the phrases of my text begin to have meaning. As a man shall say, I believe in God, and I believe that I am indeed in His likeness and image, of His very being, offspring of Deity, and I am approaching the bound of life where the burdens of time are laid down, coming to the hour in which I pass out into the nakedness of my essential life into the very presence of God, and I am unprepared. Then he inquires, Is there any way by which I can be prepared? Is there any way by which I can overtake the tragedy of lost years and expended strength? Is there any way by which I can be born anew? Nicodemus' difficulty was not a surface difficulty: "How can a man be born when he is old? Can he enter a second time into his mother's womb, and be born?" That is, can he force himself back through the years and undo the things that have been done, and change the set and tendency of his life? Can he begin again? That is the great cry of the human soul when the soul comes to consciousness of God, of its own spiritual nature, of the fact that this life is transient, probationary, and that the revolving wheels of time are bearing it ever closer to the moment when it stands alone in the presence of the God from whom it came. The Christian evangel is the answer to that cry.

What, then, is the way of salvation? We may omit from our consideration from this moment forward the man who has no sense of sin. I would do it respectfully, reverently, but I would say earnestly to that man, From now on I have no message for you. I am here as the messenger of my Master, and He Himself said: "I came not to call the righteous, but sinners to repentance."

What, then, shall I do to be saved? some soul is asking. It may be that the soul that asks will never utter those words in my hearing, will never make application with this great spiritual inquiry to any prophet, priest, or teacher. It is a question of the inner life. What, then, shall I do to be saved? The great phrases of the apostle are the perfect and final answer, "Repentance toward God, and faith toward our Lord Jesus Christ."

If we are to understand such simple phrases as these we must approach them in the simplest way. What is repentance? That is the first inquiry. Repentance is not self-reformation. Repentance is not sorrow for sin. Repentance is a change of mind, and a change of mind when it is true and deep necessarily and inevitably issues in change of attitude and change of conduct. The word of my text does not suggest sorrow—do not misunderstand me, I am not saying that repentance is unaccompanied by sorrow, but I want you to clearly understand that repentance is not sorrow. I have known men and women who have truly repented toward God, who at the moment had no deep sorrow for sin, but it came, and it grew and deepened with the passing years. I venture to affirm most solemnly, as a matter of profound conviction, that there are men who have been following the Lord Jesus Christ for half a century whose sorrow for sin is profounder now than when they commenced the Christian life. On the other hand, I have known men who have been genuinely sorry for sin but have not repented. There may be contrition, there may be lamenting over the thing done that cannot be undone, there may be the agony that cries out with Lady Macbeth,

> Out damned spot!
> Not all the perfumes of Araby
> will sweeten this little hand.

Yet there may be no repentance. Repentance is a change of mind. That is fundamental. The changed conception always expresses itself in change of attitude, and the change of attitude produces change of conduct. So that ultimately repentance is turning the back deliberately on everything that is out of harmony with the will of God. Fundamentally it is turning to God. This same apostle, in one of the first, perhaps the very first, of his letters, that to the Thessalonians, gives a remarkable description of the commencement of the Christian life, "Ye turned to God from idols, to serve a living and true God, and to wait for His Son from heaven." In that description you have an exact account of what repentance is. It is turning to God.

But here is our difficulty. Let me say it with all the faithfulness of which I am capable: it is the peculiar difficulty of such a congregation as this. I have preached to congregations to whom the matter is understood in a moment, a congregation of men and women in the depths. It was quite easy to talk to them about repentance; such sinners understand that repentance means turning around and facing God. The difficulty in such an audience as this is that faces look up into the face of the preacher and say, Why emphasize this? We are not turned from God. But are we not turned from God? Godlessness has many manifestations. It is not the peculiar quality of the penitentiary. It is found in the university. It does not dwell alone in the slum. It is found in the suburb. It is not peculiar to vulgarized humanity. It is the more subtle wrong of cultured humanity.

Godlessness! What is godlessness? Leaving God out of account in all the actualities of life. Intellectual search that does not take account of Him. Emotional outgoing that does not seek the purifying of His fire. Especially, the central volitional activity of choice that never thinks of Him until the choice is made. Life that lives as though there were no God and yet occasionally confesses God is godless. The man who conducts his business six days a week as though there were no God and comes here and worships, profanes the sanctuary and blasphemes. Repentance is turning around and facing God, recognizing the throne, submitting thereto, asking at the gates of the high place for the orders of every day and every hour. That is godly life. Repentance is toward God, the change of the mind back toward Him, that He may be taken into account; the change of the conduct so that it may square with that master conception of life that the will of God is supreme.

Let me say, further, that repentance is induced by the ministry of the Holy Spirit, but that repentance depends entirely on the choice of the human soul. It is induced by the Spirit. The Spirit of God induces repentance in the heart of a man by revealing to him the true nature of his sin, by revealing to him the attitude of God toward sin and toward himself. By the proclamation of the Evangel, by the enunciation of the Divine ethic, the Spirit induces man toward repentance. The Spirit reveals to man what sin is, showing him that sin mars the life, that no man can come to fulfillment of his own life who forgets God; that, because the very forces of life are God-created forces and life cannot come to highest realization or fullest meaning save within His will and under His law, sin therefore spoils the life. The Spirit reveals to man that such sin spreads insidiously. The forgetting of God which is casual becomes the forgetting of God which is habitual.

> Trailing clouds of glory do we come
> From God who is our home,

and the little child, granted that its surroundings are what they ought to be, is familiar with God. How wonderfully familiar a little child is with God, but with the passing of the days there is, first, the casual forgetfulness, the failure to recognize God in the hour of volitional choice, then the forgetfulness that hardens into a habit until God is shut out of life, and the finest things of life are blunted, spoiled. The Spirit brings home to man this sense of failure.

I know the things whereof I speak; I know them in my experience, and I know them in this ministry of dealing with men and women personally that God has committed to me. Not many days ago a cultured, refined man, brilliant in scholarship, looked into my eyes, and I never shall forget the look of haunting fear on his face as he said, "Oh God, what a failure I am!" It was the sense of sin, of the spoiled life. I am inclined to think that this man might have said with the rich young ruler of old, in the presence of every commandment in the second table of the decalogue, I have broken none of them. It was the sense of failure that swept his soul. The Spirit of God thus brings a man—to use an old phrase, the phrase of our fathers, may it come to us with power—to conviction of sin.

The Spirit of God comes revealing to man not merely what sin is and that he is a sinner, but also revealing the attitude of God toward sin and the attitude of God toward the sinner. What has the Spirit to say concerning God's attitude toward sin? "Thou that art of purer eyes than to behold evil, and that canst not look on perverseness." What has the Spirit to say about God's attitude toward sinners? "God so loved the world, that He gave His only begotten Son, that whosoever believeth on Him should not perish, but have eternal life." The attitude of God toward sin is that of relentless hostility, because sin spoils man. God's attitude toward the sinner is that of love stronger than death, mightier than the grave, so infinite and wonderful and profound that it stoops to the level of the ruined man, and, gathering to itself all the pain and agony resulting from sin, cancels it in the passion of His own heart.

This ministry of unveiling the Spirit induces repentance, but if repentance be induced by the work of the Spirit it must be a human act. Here is the realm of tragedy. Men come to this point, the Spirit revealing the fact of sin to them—not always in the hour of Christian worship, sometimes suddenly unexpectedly, right in the midst of daily business, sometimes in the presence of a great bereavement, sometimes when hope is springing within them and some new joy is coming to them—and, tragedy of all tragedies, there are men who do not respond to the Spirit and decline to repent, and turn back again to the beggarly elements of sin. For the advantage of the moment, for the supposed advantage of the moment, they shut out the vision of the infinite and bend themselves to the immediate. That is what some of you have done over and over again.

Yet we must go further. A man repenting is not a man saved. I may turn my back on sin and my face toward God, resolutely and with determination; but something more is needed. Change of attitude does not undo the past, neither can it alter the nature. Given a man repenting in answer to the Spirit's illumination, what does he really need? What he needs most of all is forgiveness, absolution. He cries for forgiveness for the past, does not believe it possible at first, cannot see how he can be forgiven; but he asks it, and I believe I interpret the deepest feeling of your heart as I speak out of my own experience and say, If you could persuade me that God simply says, We will say no more about the past— then I want more than that! I want loosing from the past, some cleansing from its defilement, I want something that shall purge me as hyssop cannot. I want some hand to blot out the past.

I need more. I want to be sure, when I turn my face to God, that He will receive me again. I who have rebelled against His throne, I want to know whether He will take me home again. I need more than that. And here is the profoundest thing of all, to me at least I want to know how I shall be able to manage tomorrow, for, so help me God, I speak out of my own experience, if salvation means simply sin forgiven, and I am left paralyzed, it is hardly worthwhile. I have to face the same temptations, Can I be enabled? I have to go back from this quiet hour in the sanctuary to the city, to hear the thousand siren voices, to be lured by the glitter of the straw in the dust! Can I be made strong so that I shall stand erect? Whether I look back or within or on, while I repent I am still a needy soul.

This sense of need is met in the apostle's second phrase: "Faith toward our Lord Jesus Christ." As he said the words, I venture to affirm that before his eyes there gleamed the glory of Christ Himself, and he saw how that Christ stands confronting the repentant soul, bringing to that soul everything for which it asks. What about this past? "Who His own self bare our sins in His body upon the tree." I had better leave it there. To try to explain that would but be to darken counsel with a multiplicity of words. To attempt to tell how in some infinite transaction in the darkness, God has made possible the blotting out of sin is beyond me and increasingly beyond me. The longer I live, the less I can understand its mystery and the more I know its power. Christ confronts the soul and says He will put His hand, His pierced hand, across the page of the past and blot it out.

What about God's acceptance of me? Christ tells me that I need have no fear in this matter, that God never turned His face away from me, it was I who turned my face away from Him. In the one matchless picture that Jesus gives us of the Father in the old familiar parable in the fifteenth chapter of Luke's gospel that fact is revealed: "While he was yet afar off, his father saw him, and ran, and fell on his neck, and kissed him." That is God. That is what Christ came to show us. Christ did not come to persuade God to love us, but to show us that God never ceased to love us. He did not come to make God change His mind; He came to make me change my mind, and to tell me that when I turn back to God, God is far more than halfway to meet me. Even the parable of Jesus breaks down—I say it reverently—for God in Christ came all the way to the far country to find me, and now

> My God is reconciled,
> His pardoning voice I hear.
> He owns me for His child;
> I can no longer fear.
> With confidence I now draw nigh,
> And Father, Abba Father, cry.

What about tomorrow? How am I to stand erect who have so often fallen by the way? How am I to master the things that so long have mastered me? Again the Christ stands before me and says, I who have blotted out your sin, I who have revealed the Father to you so that you may know His face is toward you still in love, "Lo, I am with thee all the days." A quaint yet beautiful story comes to my mind. To an old Scotsman his master said one day: "Donald, I am going to give you that little cottage and bit of land for your own." The Scotsman looked into the face of his master and said, "Master, I don't think I want it." "Why not?" "Well, I have saved nothing, and I can't stock it, and I can't work it." "Oh," said the master, "I think we can arrange that. I will invest a little capital, and give you the stock." The man looked up into his master's face and said, "If it's you and me together for it I think we can manage." Christ says, I give you back your birthright, I bring you back to God, blot out your sin, readmit you to the fellowship that you turned your back upon. I say, I am afraid, I am weak, I have failed! He says, "I am with you all the days." Then, reverently employing my parable, I say, With Christ I can. "I can do all things through Christ which strengtheneth me." If He will be with me in the coming days, then verily I can.

Faith is more than intellectual assent to the accuracy of a gospel. It is the venture of the soul on the Gospel. Here is a check. I hold it in my hand signed. I believe in that check; but I really believe in it when I endorse it and cash it. Here is an enterprise. I believe in it. I really believe in it when I share in its processes. Then join it, and we shall know you believe in it.

> Venture on Him, venture wholly,
> Let no other trust intrude.

Look into the eyes of Christ and say, I repent, I turn to God, I come, oh, Christ, to You. I trust in Your promise. I yield myself to Your command. Lead on, and I will follow You. That is faith.

Wherever a man shall thus venture on the word of this Christ, having faith toward Him, having repented toward God, then life begins anew. If the vessel has been marred in the hand of the Potter, He will make it again another vessel.

NOTES

High Time to Awake Out of Sleep

Robert Murray McCheyne (1813–1843) is one of the brightest lights of the Church of Scotland. Born in Dundee, he was educated in Edinburgh and licensed to preach in 1835. For a brief time, he assisted his friend Andrew A. Bonar at Larbert and Dunipace. In 1836 he was ordained and installed as pastor of St. Peter's Church, Dundee, where he served until his untimely death two months short of his thirtieth birthday. He was known for his personal sanctity and his penetrating ministry of the Word, and great crowds came to hear him preach. *The Memoirs of and Remains of Robert Murray McCheyne*, by Andrew Bonar, is a Christian classic that every minister of the gospel should read.

This sermon, preached April 2, 1840, is taken from *A Basket of Fragments*, published in Aberdeen, Texas, by James Murray.

Robert Murray McCheyne

3

HIGH TIME TO AWAKE OUT OF SLEEP

> And that, knowing the time, that now it is high time to awake out of sleep, now is our salvation nearer than when we believed (Romans 12:11).

IN THESE WORDS, Paul tells believers that it is waking time; and I would just tell you, dear friends, the same. It is high time for you to awake out of sleep. There is a condition among Christians which may be called sleeping; like the ten virgins, they slumber and sleep. Ah! I fear there are many sleeping Christians among you. It is waking time, believer. Do you know what time it is? You do not seem to know how near sunrise it is.

I will now show you what it is to be *sleeping Christians*. It is to be one that has come to Christ, yet has fallen asleep in sin. Like the church at Ephesus, they have left their first love: They do not retain that realization of Christ's preciousness—that freshness of believing. They have forgotten the fresh grasp of a Savior. So it is with some among yourselves. You may have seen your sins; yet you have lost that fresh conviction of sin you once felt so deeply. You do not see such a beauty in Jesus. The more we look at Him, just the more we would look again. Earthly things pall upon the taste; but it is not so with things divine—they grow sweeter the more often you use them. So every time you look at Jesus, He grows more precious. The rose is sweet, yet it loses its smell; but the lovely Rose of Sharon grows sweeter and sweeter. Earthly apples lose their taste; but the apple tree does not so— "Stay me with flagons, comfort me with apples, for I am sick of love." Sleepy Christians, you have lost taste for the apples. Oh! it is not time for you to sleep any longer. Believer, if you sleep on, you will soon doubt if ever you have come to Christ at all.

To awake out of sleep, then, is to see that *divine things are realities.* When you are half asleep, you see things imperfectly. Ah! you are not affected by divine realities. Now, what is it to awake out of sleep? To awake out of sleep is to see sin as it is—your heart as it is—Christ as He is—and the love of God in Christ Jesus. And you can see all this by looking to Calvary's Cross. O! it is an awful thing to look to the Cross and not be affected, nor feel conviction of sin—nor feel drawn to Christ. O! I do not know a more sad state than this. O! pray that you may be wide awake. Dear friends, our life is like a river, and we are like a boat sailing down that river. We are drawing nearer and nearer to the shores of eternity. Some may have believed for forty years. Ah! your salvation is nearer than when you first believed. Your redemption draws nigh—the redemption of your whole soul—your complete redemption. And the time is coming when we will get it—you will be saved, and then the last stone will be put on with shoutings of "Grace! grace! unto it." Then will the crown be put upon your heads, for you will be more than conquerors.

Dear friends, I do not know how far the day is spent. This is a dark, dark time; but the day is breaking—the shadows are fleeing away. The river Euphrates is drying up—that shows the day is breaking. The Jews, God's ancient people, are bringing in, and that shows the day is far spent.

And it is also high time for *unconverted men to awake out of sleep.* O, sinners! you are fast asleep, you are lying dormant—dead. O, sleepy souls, it is high time you should awake. Do you know what angels said when they went to and fro upon the earth? They told the Lord, "Behold, all the earth sitteth still and is at rest." Ah! you are fast asleep. God has given you the spirit of slumber. Do you not remember the message to Amos—"Woe to them that are at ease in Zion?" And that is the case with many of you. When you come to this house, you are in a place where Jesus has called sleepy souls, and where He has been found of very many. O, sleeping souls; it is high time for you to awake. You are living in a dream. Every

Christless man will find at last that he has been dreaming. Ah! the time is coming when you shall find that your following after gold is but a golden dream. And is there no pleasure in a dream? Who has not felt that there is pleasure even in dreams. But, ah! you must awake. Like a man condemned to die (and many of you are condemned already), he dreams of home, of his wife and children, of freedom and pleasure; but, ah! he awakes by the toll of the death-bell, and he finds that—behold it was but a dream!

Now, unconverted men, you are taking a sleep; but, like the man, you will awake from a bright dream to a bitter reality. Dear friends, I often think when I look to your houses as I pass along, and when I look in your faces, that ministers are like watchmen—they see the fire and they give the alarm. Many of you are in danger as one in a burning house. Sometimes you wonder at our anxiety for you. Sometimes you say, "Why are you so harsh?" O, poor soul! It is because the house is on fire. O, then, can we speak too harshly?—can we knock too loudly at the door of your consciences? I remember what a woman once told John Newton on her deathbed. She said, "You often spoke to me of Christ; but O! you did not tell me enough about my danger." O! I fear many of you will tell me the same. O! I fear many may reproach me on a deathbed, or in hell, that I did not tell you more often that there was a hell. Would to God I had none to reproach me at last; God help me to speak to you plainly. It is high time to awake out of sleep, sinner: for now your damnation slumbers not. Dear friends, it is now more than three years since I first spoke to you, though it just seems like a day since I first came beseeching you to be reconciled to God—beseeching you to come to Jesus. Every day that passes is bringing you nearer to the judgment seat. Not one of you is standing still. You may sleep; but the tide is going on, bringing you nearer death, judgment, and eternity.

Dear friends, another reason for awaking is, *your condemnation is still getting greater and greater.* When I first came among you your guilt was not so great as now.

"Despisest thou the riches of his goodness, and forbear-
ance, and long-suffering; not knowing that the goodness
of God leadeth thee to repentance; but after thy hardness
and impenitent heart, treasurest up unto thyself wrath
against the day of wrath, and revelation of the righteous
judgment of God?" (Rom. 2:4–5). Do any of you know that
you are treasuring up wrath against the day of wrath?
You are laying up in the bank. You are laying up wrath
for a coming eternity. Will this not convince you that it is
high time to awake out of sleep? It is time tonight to put
on the Lord Jesus. It is high time, sleeper. It is the very
time. Will you not awake? Ah! I can tell you one thing—
you will find it all true at last, that you have treasured up
wrath against the day of wrath. Every sin is a drop of
wrath; which, like a river dammed up, gets deeper and
deeper and fuller, until at last it bursts forth. O! are there
not many misers of wrath here? Do you not see that it is
high time for you to awake out of sleep before you have an
infinity of wrath laid up? Awake now, and it may be all
taken away. There is one ready to take it away if you will
but apply to Him. Sinner! Awake!

Another reason is, that *opportunities of awaking are
passing away.* Now, I do say there are times of awaking.
There is a time when the ark is passing by your houses; if
you allow it to pass, you will find one day, when you
would step in, that you will be overcome by the angry
waters. You remember the little man of Jericho, Zaccheus.
Jesus was passing through Jericho on His way to Jerusalem to be crucified. It was the last time He was to pass
that way; it was the last time Zaccheus could see the
Savior. When Jesus was to pass, lest he should be lost
among the crowd, he climbed up into a sycamore tree.
Jesus passed, looked up, and said, "Zaccheus, come down;
for today I must abide at thy house." O! had he not come
down that moment from the sycamore tree—had he not
made haste and come down—he would have come down
and gone to a lost eternity. Had he not that hour closed
with Jesus, he would have gone to that place where there
is no voice of mercy, for Jesus passed by for the last time.
And I do say, sinner, if you do not come down from your

sycamore tree, and receive Christ tonight, you may not be permitted tomorrow. Now is the accepted time. O! come to Him *now*. O! you will rejoice forever if you entertain Him joyfully tonight. Sleepy sinner! now awake. It is high time to awake; for the time is at hand when there will be no Bible—no more offers of mercy. We have many precious ordinances now, but they will all come to an end. Our Thursday evenings will soon come to an end too. O! make haste, then, and come down, and Jesus this night will abide in your house. He is saying, "Behold I stand at the door and knock. If any man hear my voice, and open the door, I will come in to him, and will sup with him, and he with me." Had Zaccheus slept, he would never have seen Jesus; if you do not awake, alas! alas! for the day comes when you shall wail because of Him. Amen.

A Revival Promise

Charles Haddon Spurgeon (1834–1892) is undoubtedly
the most famous minister of the last century. Converted
in 1850, he united with the Baptists and soon began to
preach in various places. He became pastor of the Baptist
church in Waterbeach in 1851, and three years later he
was called to the decaying Park Street Church, London.
Within a short time the work began to prosper, a new
church was built and dedicated in 1861, and Spurgeon
became London's most popular preacher. In 1855, he began
to publish his sermons weekly; today they make up the
fifty-seven volumes of *The Metropolitan Tabernacle Pulpit*.
He founded a pastor's college and several orphanages.

   This sermon is taken from *The Metropolitan Tabernacle
Pulpit*, Volume 20.

Charles Haddon Spurgeon

4

A REVIVAL PROMISE

For I will pour water upon him that is thirsty, and floods upon the dry ground: I will pour my spirit upon thy seed, and my blessing upon thine offspring: and they shall spring up as among the grass, as willows by the water courses. One shall say, I am the Lord's; and another shall call himself by the name of Jacob; and another shall subscribe with his hand unto the Lord and surname himself by the name of Israel (Isaiah 44:3–5).

IN THE CHRISTIAN CHURCH at this moment there is a very general desire for a revival of religion. You may go where you may among Christian people, and you will find that they are mourning over the present state of things, and saying the one to the other, "When will a greater blessing come? How can we obtain it? When shall we make some impression upon the masses of the ungodly? When shall our houses of prayer be filled with attentive hearers? When will the Lord's kingdom come, and his right arm be made bare in the eyes of all the people?" I am delighted to hear the inquiry; my soul magnifies the Lord as I discern tokens of growing anxiety about the cause and kingdom of Jesus and the perishing sons of men. This is an omen of better times. "As soon as Zion travailed, she brought forth her children." Searchings of heart, anguish, groanings which cannot be uttered, and abounding intercession, are the heralds of blessing; they are that sound in the tops of the mulberry trees which calls upon believers to bestir themselves in hope of victory. May the movement among the saints continue and deepen, until it brings forth a movement among sinners far and wide.

At this time, also, there are manifest the most pleasing signs that God is about to work among His people. A very notable ingathering of converts has taken place in the town of Newcastle, and the two brethren whom God honored to be the means of it have now removed to the city of Edinburgh. There the ministers of all denominations are united in helping them, and in earnestly imploring the divine blessing; the gracious visitation which has already come upon Edinburgh is such as was probably never known before within the memory of man. The whole place seems to be moved from end to end. When we hear of many thousands coming together on weekdays to quite ordinary meetings, and crying, "What must we do to be saved?" there is, we are persuaded, the hand of God in the matter. Now, there is among earnest Christians a general feeling that what has been done for Edinburgh is greatly needed for London, and must be done for London, if prayer and earnest effort can obtain it. Our prayers must go up incessantly that God will be pleased to send forth His saving health among the people of this great city of four million souls, and turn many to righteousness, to the praise of the glory of His grace. Our growing anxiety for Christ's glory and our faith in the energy of His Spirit will be two hopeful signs of a coming blessing.

As a church we have always felt a delight in any work of this kind that has to be done for God, and we have enjoyed for many years a continuous visitation of grace. That which would be a revival anywhere else has been our ordinary condition, for which we are thankful. By the space of these twenty years, almost without rise or fall, God has continued to increase our numbers with souls saved by the preaching of His truth. To Him be all the praise! But now we are anxious to take a part in a yet further advance; we want a greater blessing. What we have had has not decreased, but rather stimulated our appetite. Oh, for more conversions! more hearts for Jesus! Would God that the dews of heaven would fall in sevenfold abundance upon us and our fellow Christians, and the past be put to the blush by the future! That this desire may be fanned to a flame in all our hearts is my earnest prayer. I have taken this text as one which is full of encouragement, that all we may be moved with hope and excited with expectation.

I shall handle it in this way. First, we have before us *the great covenant blessing of the church*; secondly, we have *the glorious result of that blessing described*; and when we have spoken thus, we shall spend the rest of our time in speaking of *the conduct which is consistent with the desire that this blessing, and its results, may come to us.*

The Great Covenant Blessing of the Church

It is the gift of the Holy Spirit. Whatever metaphor is used, this is the meaning of it. He is the refreshing, life-giving, fertilizing water, the living water of which Jesus spoke. The first promise of the text, "I will pour water upon him that is thirsty, and floods upon the dry ground," is explained by the second, "I will pour my spirit upon thy seed, and my blessing upon thine offspring."

While speaking upon this, it is well for us to remember, first, that *this blessing has been already given*. We must never underrate the importance of the ascension of our Lord, and the gift of the Spirit which followed thereupon. God forbid that we should think lightly of Pentecost: the Holy Spirit then descended, and we have no record that the Spirit has since ascended and departed from the church. He is the church's perpetual heritage, and abides with us forever. I like to sing—

> The Holy Ghost is here,
> Where saints in prayer agree.
> As Jesu's parting gift he's near
> Each pleading company.
>
> Not far away is he,
> To be by prayer brought nigh,
> But here in present majesty,
> As in his courts on high.

He is permanently resident in the midst of the church. But when we have received that truth, we may still go on to use the language which is very frequent among us, and pray for the outpouring of the Spirit. If the language be not exactly accurate, the meaning is most excellent. So far as any one assembly or person is concerned, we may request the Holy Spirit to be poured forth upon us in His gracious operations; we desire to see the Spirit of God working more mightily in the church; we long each one of us to be more completely subject to His influences, and more filled with His power, so that we may be full of faith and of the Holy Spirit. We want to see the Holy Spirit poured upon those who have it not; upon the dead in sin that they may be quickened, upon the desponding that they may be consoled, upon the ignorant that they may be illuminated, and upon seekers that they may find Him who alone is our peace. We, being evil, give good gifts to our children, and therefore we are persuaded that our heavenly Father will give the Holy Spirit to them that ask Him. We do but enlarge upon the prayer of the apostolic benediction when we cry for the blessing peculiar to the Holy Spirit. It is the Spirit that quickens; neither the letter of the Word nor the energy of our manner can give life; therefore we feel that when we have prophesied to the dry bones we must also prophesy to the wind; for unless the breath divine shall come, the dry bones will never live.

Notice, beloved, that this great covenant blessing of the Spirit is in our text *the subject of a promise.* "I will pour water upon him that is thirsty, and floods upon the dry ground; I will pour my Spirit upon thy seed, and my blessing upon thine offspring." We may always be confident of receiving those blessings which are promised by the Lord. The general promise, "No good thing will I withhold from them that walk uprightly," is very comforting. Under its broad cover we are encouraged to plead for many favors for which we have no special note of promise. But when we can put our finger upon a plain and specific word, by which a certain good thing is guaranteed to us, our faith rises to full assurance and we feel confident of receiving an answer to our prayer. "Thou hast said, 'I will pour my spirit upon thy seed,' therefore, O Lord, fulfill this word unto thy servant, in which thou hast caused him to hope." You have God's word for it; place your finger upon it, and on your knees beseech the Lord to do as He has said. He cannot lie, He never will revoke His word. Has He said, and shall He not do it?

As well might he his being quit,
As break his promise or forget.

He has spontaneously made the promise, and He will divinely make it good. Upon every promise the blood of Jesus Christ has set its seal, making it "yea and amen" forever. Prove Him, then, herewith, and you shall find Him faithfulness itself. A promise of God is the essence of truth, the soul of certainty, the voice of faithfulness, and the substance of blessing.

What a right royal promise it is! How lofty and full of assurance is the language! "I will pour water upon him that is thirsty." It is for God to say, "I will" and "I will." We may venture as far as declaring, "I will if I can"; but there are no limits to His power. Our wisdom is to say, "I hope I shall be able to do as I desire"; but there are no impossibilities with the Almighty. His Spirit falls upon men as a dew from the Lord, waiting not for man, neither tarrying for the sons of men. When the time has come for a shower, God asks not the potentates of earth to give their consent, but down come the blessed drops. When the season for spring has arrived, the Lord does not ask man to help Him to remove the ice from the streams, or the snow from the hills, or the damps from the air. He asks no human aid in quickening the seeds, and arousing the plants, so that the sleeping flowers may open their lovely eyes and smile on all around. He does it all. His mystic influences, as omnipotent as they are secret, come forth and the work is done. And so, glory be to God, we have a promise here which is the word of omnipotence. When we plead it we need not be at all dismayed by the question, "Can such a thing be?" We know that dry bones can live when the Spirit breathes upon them, and we are equally well persuaded that the life-giving Spirit can so breathe, for we have a divine promise that He shall be given to the people. We hear the double "I will, I will," and we are certain that the Lord can and will "pour water upon him that is thirsty, and floods upon the dry ground."

It becomes us also, brethren, to notice that this gift, which is the subject of a promise, is *a most needful blessing.*

I have sometimes heard it sneeringly remarked that we know very well we want the Holy Spirit, and there is no need to be everlastingly talking about it. But, brethren, we need to make frequent acknowledgment of this truth. It is due to the Holy Spirit Himself that we should do so. If we do not honor the Holy Spirit, we cannot expect Him to work with us. He will be grieved, and leave us to find out our helplessness. Moreover, I fear that, however generally the doctrine of the necessity of the Spirit's work may be believed as a matter of theory, it is not acted upon; and what is not believed in practice is in fact not believed at all. I am very suspicious of a man who tires of a truth so vitally important, and dares to call it a platitude. We shall not hesitate to repeat the doctrine again and again, and we feel persuaded that God's people will not tire of it. Without the Spirit of God we can do nothing; we are as ships without wind, or chariots without steeds; like branches without sap, we are withered; like coals without fire, we are useless; as an offering without the sacrificial flame, we are unaccepted. I desire both to feel and to confess this fact whenever I attempt to preach. I do not wish to get away from it, or to conceal it, nor can I, for I am often made to feel it to the deep humbling of my spirit.

I pray that you who teach in the Sunday school, you who visit the poor, you who work in any way for God, may own your impotence for good, and look for power from on high. To our hand the Holy Spirit is the force, to our eye He is the light. We are but the stones and He the sling, we are the arrows and He the bow. Confess your weakness, and you will be fit to be strengthened; own your emptiness, and it will be a preparation for receiving the divine fullness. For, observe, the promise of the living water is to "him that is thirsty," or, as it may be better rendered, and the figure would be more clear, "I will pour water upon it (the land) that is thirsty, and floods upon the dry ground." The blessing is to come where it is needed, upon the desert, the parched places which are as the valley of death until the rain comes. If you think yourself to be as the well-watered plain of Sodom, God will pour no floods upon you. It is upon the thirsty land, upon the heart which laments its barrenness, and confesses its own unworthiness, that the Spirit of God shall come. I do pray that as a church we may never imbibe the idea that we have an entail of God's blessing, or a monopoly of His benediction; so that He is sure to append His approval to any one particular ministry, or any form of church government. The Lord might leave us, and will unless we lie low before Him and own our nothingness. Remember His word which He spoke to His erring people when they boasted of their pedigree and called themselves His temple: "Go ye now unto my place which was in Shiloh, where I set my name at the first, and see what I did to it for the wickedness of my people Israel." He may leave His garden to be overgrown with briers, and His vineyard to be marred with stones. God is not tied to any one place or people, He can remove the candlestick and set it up in another chamber; let the seven churches of Asia Minor serve as a warning to us in this thing. Blessed Spirit of the living God, we do confess the barrenness of our soil, and the drought of our land, and we beseech You never to withdraw Your dew, or cause Your rain to depart from us! What greater curse could You inflict than to let us alone? Oh, come upon us, we beseech You, and let the divine promise be fulfilled!

It should be very comfortable to us to reflect that, while we need the Spirit of God, *His working is most effectual* to supply all our needs when He does come upon us. In the east, you can generally tell where there is a stream or a river by the line of emerald which marks it. If you stood on a hill, you could see certain lines of green, made up of grass, reeds, rushes, and occasional trees, which have sprung up along the water courses. Nothing is required to make the land fertile but to water it. We are told by travelers that they have seen plains looking completely barren, apparently covered with dry dust and powder; yet a heavy shower has fallen, and in a space of time which seems incredible in our colder climate, the most lovely flowers and the most refreshing verdure have clothed the plains, until the wilderness and the solitary places have been glad, and the desert has rejoiced and blossomed as the rose. Yes, it has blossomed exceedingly, and an excellency as of Carmel and Sharon has been upon it. Even thus let the Spirit of God come upon any church, and it is all that it needs to make it living and fruitful. Church machinery, apart from the Spirit of God, lacks the motive power; the motive power coming, your machinery will do its work. Of course, if it is an imperfect machinery, the Holy Spirit will not make it do all the work which a better organization would have done; still, even the most imperfect shall accomplish so much as to astonish all who behold it. What a blessing it is when the church does really receive the Spirit of God abundantly! Her ministry may be slow in utterance; like Moses, the leader of the people may be a man of stammering speech; or, like Paul, his personal appearance may be mean, and his speech contemptible; but this matters nothing when the Spirit of God is upon the man and in the people. The church may be very small, and the members may be very poor, and many of them illiterate, too; but as the barley cake of the soldier's dream smote the royal pavilion of Midian, so that it lay along, so the Lord, by the hand of the feeblest, shall do His greatest deeds, and get to Himself renown. Where the Spirit of God is, there is the majesty of omnipotence.

I here call your attention to the fact that the promise in our text is *liberal and unstinted.* "I will *pour* water upon the thirsty land, and *floods* upon the dry ground." The Lord does not need to stint His gifts. When He gives a blessing He gives it like a king. His treasury will not be exhausted by giving, or replenished by withholding. I have seen in Italy the fields watered by the processes of irrigation: there are trenches made to run along the garden, and smaller gutters to carry the lesser streams to each bed, so that each plant gets its share of water; but the husbandman has to be very careful, for he has but little water in his tank, and only an allotted share of the public reservoir. No plant must have too much. No plot of ground must be drenched. How different is this from the methods of the Lord! He pours the water. He deluges the land.

"The parched ground shall become a pool, and the thirsty land springs of water; in the habitation of dragons, where each lay, shall be grass with reeds and rushes." Oh that He would pull up the floodgates now, and let a torrent of grace rush through this Tabernacle. Oh that at this moment He would open the windows of heaven, and send us a flood of grace, like the deluge of vengeance in Noah's day, until the tops of our loftiest expectations should be covered. He is able to do exceeding abundantly above what we ask, or even think. He gives liberally, and upbraids not. Our abounding sin and death need abounding life and power. In such a city as this the largest blessing will be none too great. Let us open our mouths wide, that He may fill them. The Lord is illimitable in His wealth of grace, and boundless in His goodness and power. Let us take the promise as it stands and plead it at the throne, "Hast thou not said, 'I will pour water upon him that is thirsty, and floods upon the dry ground'?" Lord, do it, to the praise of the glory of Your grace.

One other remark, and I leave this point. This covenant blessing is, in our text, *peculiarly promised to a certain class of persons who are especially dear to us.* "I will pour my spirit upon thy seed, and my blessing upon thine offspring." Parents, lay hold greedily upon these points of the promise. I am afraid we do not think enough of the promise which the Lord has made to our children. Grace does not run in the blood; we have never fallen into the gross error of birthright membership, or the supposition that the child of godly parents has a right to Christian ordinances. We know that religion is a personal matter, and is not of blood nor of birth; we know also that all children are heirs of wrath until the grace of God regenerates them; but still there is some meaning in that gracious saying, "The promise is unto you and your children, even to as many as the Lord your God shall call." Paul was assuredly not wrong, but sweetly right, when he said to the jailer, in answer to his question, "What must I do to be saved?" "Believe on the Lord Jesus Christ and thou shalt be saved, and thy house." Lay hold of those words, Christian parents, and do not be content to get half the promise. Pray to God to fulfill it all. Go to Him this very day, you mothers and fathers, and implore Him to have pity upon your offspring. Cry to Him, and say, "Thou hast said, 'I will pour my spirit on thy seed, and my blessing on thine offspring:' do it, Lord, for Jesus Christ's sake."

The Glorious Result of This Covenant Blessing

The certain result of the outpouring of the Spirit is the upspringing of spiritual life. Wherever the water comes in Palestine, as I said before, the grass will be sure to follow it, and vegetation becomes lively at once. Wherever the Spirit of God comes, there will be life in the church and life in the ministry, life in prayer, life in effort, life in holiness, life in brotherly love.

The next effect will be seen in the calling out of numerous converts by the Holy Spirit. "They shall spring up as among the grass, and as willows by the water courses." Who can count the blades of grass? They are a fine symbol of the greatness of number, and might as justly be used for that purpose as the sands of the seashore. Where the Spirit of the Lord comes, converts are not few as the cedars of Lebanon, but they flourish like the grass of the earth. They fly as a cloud, and as doves to their dovecotes. Can we be satisfied with having in a year a dozen or so added to the church? Yet I do meet with some of my brethren—and far be it from me to judge them—who say they have had a happy year, and are very comfortable though they have had only three or four persons added to the church. Surely, however small the congregation, that must be a very unsatisfactory reward for a twelvemonth's ministry. My brethren, where at this day do we see results attending the gospel which should satisfy us? Hundreds may be added to the church in a year, as has been our common blessing, but what are hundreds? If four hundred were brought into our fellowship last year, what is that out of four million? What are these saved ones among so many? The headway made by the church is next to nothing; it hardly keeps pace with the growth of the population. We want more of the Spirit of God, and if we had it, I have no doubt whatever the converts would at once be counted by thousands and tens of thousands. There is no reason whatsoever why the church of God, which is now in a pitiful minority, should not become in many a district a triumphant majority, and the influences of the grace of God be felt far and near.

Observe that the text tells us that the converts called out by the Spirit of God are vigorous and lively. "They shall spring as the grass." Now the grass in the east springs up without any sowing, cultivating, or any other attention: it comes up of itself from the fruitful soil. There is the water, and there is the grass. So where the Spirit of God is with a church there are sure to be conversions, it cannot be otherwise. True, we are bound to use all agencies that are fit and right for the promotion of the good end; but where the Spirit of God is we shall often be astonished to find that far beyond the usual result of agencies the life has extended.

The willows also are mentioned, to indicate great vitality. How rapidly the willow grows! There is a proverb in Cambridgeshire that a willow will buy a horse, where an oak won't buy a saddle, because the willow grows so quickly and yields such frequent boughs to the cutter. You may cut it this year, and in a short time you may remove its pliant boughs again, for they will come anew. So truly saved ones will bear discouragement and trial, and still spring up. If you cut every bough from the willow tree it will be green again next spring, and if you even fell it down to the root it does not signify, at the scent of water it will bud. Do you not remember when you were children taking little twigs of willow to make hoops around your little garden? You thought them dead, and therefore used them as a little fence; in a short time, to your astonishment, they were all sprouting out with green. The willow is full of life. Now, where the Spirit of God is, the newly converted are full of life. You may check them, but they will not be repressed. You orthodox people, who happen to have surly tempers, may go around with your pocket-knives and snip at their boughs cruelly, and say, "We do not want these young people; we do not want revivals," but they will grow in spite of you. Blessed be God, you elder brethren cannot turn the penitent prodigals out of doors. Should you even be so unkind to the newly grown willows as to cut them right down, they will spring up again, for if they are plants of the Lord's own right hand planting, and of the Spirit's watering, they will outlive the worst of usage. They will grow as the grass and as willows by the water courses. We may expect then, if the Spirit of God shall work among us, that there will be an abundance of converts, and those of the most vigorous kind.

These conversions will come from all quarters. The text says, one shall say, and another shall call, and another shall subscribe. Here is one who is the son of a deacon—we expected him to give his heart to Jesus. There is another, he is not the child of a religious professor, but comes right out from an ungodly family. Ah, here is another, he had grown up and come to ripe years, having followed after folly, and confirmed himself in sin, yet he comes forward, for the grace of God has called him. One comes from the wealthy, another comes from the poor, a third comes from nobody knows where; they will and must come, for God knows His own, and will call them. They shall come from all trades and occupations, from all churches and denominations; from these little boys below me, I hope, and from you gray-headed people over yonder—one here, another there. We shall be wonder-struck as we hear from all corners, and parts, and places, "I am the Lord's"; and again, "I am called by the name of Jacob"; and again, "I am surnamed this day by the name of Israel." The work of divine grace does not run in a groove, but breaks out where it seems least likely to do so. At one time it creates a revival at Samaria, at another time it saves a widow at Joppa or the eunuch on the road to Gaza. Lord call whomsoever You will, but do call many, for Jesus' sake.

One memorable thing about the conversions wrought by the Holy Spirit is this, that these converted people shall be led to avow their faith. They shall not, like Nicodemus, come to Jesus by night; they shall not hope to go to heaven creeping all the way behind the hedge; they shall avow their allegiance. "One shall say, I am the Lord's; and another shall call himself by the name of Jacob, and another shall subscribe with his hand unto the Lord, and surname himself by the name of Israel." The God of Israel shall be their God and the people of Israel shall be their people. I love to see both these things in young converts. Some appear to dedicate themselves to God, but they feel themselves such superior beings that they do not join with any church. They hold themselves in the isolation which practically means, "Stand by, I am holier than thou." They do not think any church good enough for them, but my private opinion is that they are not good enough for any church. On the other hand, some will join a church, but do not seem to have had enough respect to the inward, vital part of religion in giving themselves up to the Lord; therefore, no church will find them to be any great gain. There must be the two together, a surrender to God and then a union with the people of God. Consider the first of these points—one shall say, "I am the Lord's." He shall confess that from head to foot, body, soul and spirit, he is not his own but Christ's. He will feel, "I have been washed in His blood; I have been pardoned all my sins, and been renewed in heart; and now I am the Lord's, and I desire to live to His praise. Tell me what I can do, and how I can serve the Lord, for I am His, and mean to be His forever." This is delightful. Oh, to hear hundreds of you saying this. I would give my life to see it.

Another convert is said to subscribe with his hand to the God of Jacob. He gives himself over to God, and he does it deliberately; as deliberately as a person who signs a deed by which he makes over an estate. He writes his name, and places his finger on the seal, and calmly says, "This is my act and deed." We do not recommend persons to write out covenants with God and sign them, they are apt to gender to bondage; we do recommend them to make such a covenant in their hearts before the Most High, saying,

' Tis done, the great transaction's done;
  I am my Lord's and he is mine:
He drew me, and I followed on,
   Charmed to obey the voice divine.

The text may have another rendering, for, if you notice, the word *with* in the text is in italics, to show that it was inserted by the translators. It might run thus: "Another shall subscribe his hand unto the Lord." This alludes to the custom which still exists, but which was more common in those days, of a servant being marked or tattooed in the hand with his master's name. So was it with soldiers; frequently when they were enthusiastic for a leader they would print his name on some part of their body, and very often upon the palms of their hands. There are constant allusions to this in the classics. We know that devout worshipers dedicated themselves to the god they worshiped, and were stamped with a secret mark. Paul alludes to this when he says, "Henceforth let no man trouble me, for I bear in my body the marks of the Lord Jesus"; as much as to say, "I am Christ's: I have had His name branded upon me." When he suffered from being scourged and beaten with rods, he called it bearing the marks of the Lord Jesus, and did as good as say, "Flog away, you will only engrave His name into my flesh, for I am Christ's." Now it would be a very superstitious and foolish thing for any man to be tattooed with the name of the Lord, or with a cross; all that such an act meant in those who did it of old we ought to mean, namely, that we are forever, and beyond recall, the property of Jesus. Our ear is bored. We are servants as long as we live to our dear Master. They may sooner kill us than lead us away from Him whose we are, and whom we serve. Who shall separate us from the love of God?

> High heaven that heard the solemn vow,
>   That vow renewed shall daily hear,
> Until in life's latest hour I bow,
>   And bless in death a bond so dear.

There was dedication to God of the fullest kind, but side by side with it went unity with the church, for the declaration, "I am the Lord's," was parallel with "calling himself by the name of Jacob." Now the name of Jacob was the first, the lower, the common name of God's people, they were the seed of Jacob. "Ah," says the man who is converted,

"I do not care what they call Christian people, they may call *me* by the same title if they will, and I will not complain. They may call us Puritans, Methodists, Ranters, Quakers, or whatever they like, I am one of them." I have read of a certain nobleman who was also a saint, that when he heard religious persons scoffed at as Puritans, he was accustomed at once to declare, "I am a Puritan too. I glory in being one of them." They felt that it was of little use to mock at him, he was too stout a soldier and too bold a speaker. It is a grand thing when a man can say in company, "It does not matter what you think of religion, I belong to such and such Christian people, and I am not ashamed of it. I know their name is a mockery, and their minister is despised, but it does not matter, I am one of them." It is mentioned, also, that one surnamed himself by the name of Israel. That was the grand name of the church in those days— Israel, the prevailing prince. We ought to feel that to be a Christian is to possess a patent of nobility second to none. Duke, earl, knight, esquire—we covet none of these; call us by the name of Christ and we have honor enough. The name of Caesar is a poor thing compared with the name of Christ. Better be owned as a disciple of Jesus than as an emperor of emperors. Oh, may the Spirit of God be poured out upon this place, that many of you may be savingly converted, and then say, "I will give myself to the Lord, and will also cast in my lot with his people; where they dwell I will dwell; where they die there would I die; their people shall be my people, since their God has become my God." Pray, dear brethren, that the promise before us may be fulfilled in this church, and in all the churches of our Lord Jesus Christ.

The Conduct Suitable If We Obtain This Blessing

First, O my brethren in Christ, if we would obtain these floods of blessing we must confess how dry, how thirsty, how wilderness-like we are. Humble yourselves, therefore, under the hand of God, and He will exalt you in due time. "He hath filled the hungry with good things, but the rich he hath sent empty away." Oh, for the spirit of humiliation throughout the church!

Next to that let us cultivate prayer. "For this will I be inquired of by the house of Israel to do it for them." If you have a man's check for a thousand pounds, it would be very wicked of you to say, "I cannot get my money, this paper is not paid," if you have never taken it to the bank; and so, if you have God's promise, and have never pleaded it, it is your own fault if you have not obtained the blessing. The very least thing God can ask of us is that we shall ask of Him. "Ask and it shall be given you: seek and ye shall find: knock and it shall be opened unto you." Plead more earnestly in private, make your prayer meetings more energetic, attend them more numerously, throw your hearts more fully into them, and God's Spirit will be surely given.

Next to that, if we want the blessing we must put forth our own personal effort. It would be a most absurd thing for a man to pray for a harvest, and neither plow nor sow. I cannot conceive anything more insulting to the majesty of God than for us to pray, and meanwhile fold our arms. It is not thus that we prove our sincerity. I desire to preach to you as if the conversion of these sinners around us depended wholly upon me, and then I delight to fall back upon the truth that it wholly depends upon the Lord God. Sunday school teachers, use the means for the conversion of your children! Try and speak personally to every one of them; if you can find opportunity, pray with them one by one alone. You will win young hearts to Jesus in that way. Try, dear friends, to get hold of individuals. You who come here continually, look out for individuals in the congregation, and endeavor to tell them what you have experienced of the love of Christ. If you cannot speak to them, write letters to them; an earnest letter is as good as a sermon. Do anything, do everything, to bring souls to Jesus. While we are working we shall find God working with us, for He is never slower than His people. If we are building, He will be the Master Builder, and will build through us. For a man to pray that he may have a safe journey, and then to go to bed, and not start from home, would be wickedness; to pray to God to convert sinners, and then not to preach or teach them the

Gospel, would be a piece of impudent mockery of God. Beloved, see to this. I cannot pause to stir you up about it, for our time is going; but I pray the Holy Spirit to stir you, that everyone here may become a soul winner.

Once more, I have a word to say to those who are not the people of God. O beloved ones, who are not saved, all our concern is about your salvation. We are always preaching and praying about you. How can you obtain saving faith? I would urge you to labor after a clear idea of your real position. O unconverted people, try to know where you are, and what you are. It might perhaps arouse you from your present indifference. If you would really and distinctly understand that you are out of Christ, condemned already, an enemy to God by wicked works, with the wrath of God abiding on you, and in danger of eternal perdition, it might startle you and lead you to desire salvation. I should think hopefully of you if I knew that you were taking stock, and estimating your condition before God. May I ask you when you get home to sit down and write, every one of you, on a piece of paper, "Saved," if you are saved, and "Condemned," if you are not a believer, for that is your condition? I want you to realize whose you are, and where you are going. When you have done so, I pray that a sense of your condition and prospects may be deepened upon your mind. Sinners, do you think enough? Do you consider enough? You are busy about a thousand things, but do you really think about your souls, death and judgment, and eternal perdition? Do you think enough about the Savior's love? Do you ponder your sin, and the blessed fact that it may be pardoned? Oh, that you would reflect, consider, and turn your whole mind to God!

But I am beating the bush. I have a much more important precept to which to exhort you. Remember, the Gospel command is, "believe in the Lord Jesus Christ, and thou shalt be saved." Every minute that you remain an unbeliever you are adding to your sin, you are increasing your iniquity and confirming yourself in condemnation. Oh, that you would believe the divine testimony concerning Jesus, for that is the object of faith! What you are asked to believe is true. He whom you are commanded to trust in is able to save you; the promise that you shall be saved if you trust is a sure and certain one. Do not, therefore, fling away your souls and despise the mercy of God. May it please the Eternal Spirit to lead you at this very moment to put your trust in Jesus Christ, and to be saved; then you will be one of those who spring as the grass, and as the willows by the streams. May God bless you, every one of you, for Jesus Christ's sake. Amen.

NOTES

A Prayer for a Revival

George W. Truett (1867–1944) was perhaps the best-known Southern Baptist preacher of his day. He pastored the First Baptist Church of Dallas, Texas, from 1897 until his death and saw it grow both in size and influence. Active in denominational ministry, Truett served as president of the Southern Baptist Convention and for five years was president of the Baptist World Alliance; but he was known primarily as a gifted preacher and evangelist. Nearly a dozen books of his sermons were published.

This sermon was taken from *We Would See Jesus*, published in 1915 by Fleming H. Revell.

George W. Truett

5

A PRAYER FOR A REVIVAL

Wilt thou not revive us again: that thy people may rejoice in thee? (Psalm 85:6).

THE TEXT IS a short prayer, but volumes of meaning are wrapped up in it. God give us tonight to pray it from the very depths of our hearts! It is a prayer for God's people. "Wilt thou not revive us again: that thy people may rejoice in thee?" David does not pray about conditions or circumstances, that these may be changed, but he prays for people, for God's people. "Wilt thou not revive us again: that thy people may rejoice in thee?" For David had learned the lesson far back in that olden time, that if there be any deep, great work of grace wrought for the world that is lost, then such work of grace will begin in the hearts of God's people. It is true and does not need to be argued that, when God's people are right, things always go well with His work, and when God's people are wrong, things go badly with His work.

It is a lesson that comes down to us through all the generations, that, going before any great, deep work of grace, God's people have waited before Him in confession of sin, in supplication for His grace, in the humbling of their hearts, in the submission of their wills to Him, that He might do for them and with them according to His holy will. That is surely the lesson that comes down to us, touching God's work and people all through the generations. There is no such thing, brethren, as any great, deep, far-reaching work of grace anywhere, if God's people do not experimentally know the mighty means of prayer touching such work of grace. All history as it touches God's people and His work in the world is the confirmation of this statement. When Israel down in Egypt prayed after the right fashion, then it was that deliverance came.

In the days of Nehemiah, when God's work had run down, and when Nehemiah, with the faithful ones about him, waited upon God for its reviving and its rebuilding, when they prayed after the right fashion, the walls of God's house went up again. It was so in the days of good King Josiah. The thing that preeminently characterized the revival for the glory of God in his time was the right waiting before God of His people. And surely the one marvelous thing about that incomparable meeting on the Day of Pentecost, the influence of which kept on in such wondrous fashion for a generation, surely the one marvelous thing about that meeting, from the human viewpoint, was, that for ten days God's people just prayed. For ten long days they tarried yonder in the quiet place, away from the crowd, waiting, with one accord, for power from on high. When will we learn the lesson, brethren, that it is time gained in all respects if we give ourselves very, very much to the blessed exercise of prayer in carrying on God's work in the world? For my part I do not believe that in any of these "revivals" or "special meetings" that we have that God is honored in them, or that people are really regenerated in them, if going through them and before them and after them there is not the moving of the hearts of God's people in prayer.

When will we rightly lay such great matter to heart? It is fundamental to the real success of all God-saving effort. And you yourselves are the witnesses that I speak the truth tonight. In your own Christian experiences, out from the past, even as I talk, there come to you the memories of the occasions when you were specially blessed of God in the winning of souls. Those mighty spiritual blessings that came to you; those days of the right hand of God; those days when you heard His stately steppings; those days when you saw His mighty Spirit pierce the hearts of sinful men and bring them down, those were the times when your own hearts were empty of their self-sufficiency, and when with a cry to God from the deepest depths of the soul, you besought Him to arise and plead His own cause, and save lost sinners for whom Christ died. You yourselves, I say, are witnesses to that same significant truth. When you have had special power with men to win them to God, it was always when you had power with God. And men do not have power with God—it is a thing unknown in His spiritual kingdom—if they be not men of prayer, men of real intercession, men who know the meaning of the secret place where alone they look into the King's face until He speaks His message to them. There is no such thing as power to win lost men to God if His people do not pray. You yourselves, I say, are witnesses to that great fact. The times when you have had power with men so that they could not resist your appeals, so that you saw their faces humbled before you, and you saw the conquest of the soul go on before your very eyes, those were the times when you were in touch with the great King, when your soul had conscious fellowship with Him, when you took hold of Him and felt that you were one with Him. Men who come to realize that experience do so through the gracious medium of prayer.

"The burden of the Lord," when that is upon them, then it is that men know the burden of prayer. O brethren, this light, easy, tearless, hop, skip and jump method in the matchless work of turning men to God is not the New Testament way. If men are turned to Almighty God in any blessed fashion, then the people of God know about it, and there is a cry to Him, the deepest cry of their hearts is heard, that lost sinners may be saved. God's people always cry like that if any mighty movement of His Spirit and His living grace is felt among the people.

When I was a little lad I recall how that again and again I went to the old country church to their appointed "protracted meetings" every summer, and the farmers would gather in at the morning meetings, and then again at the evening meetings, two services a day, and they would thus daily gather together for several days. Great crowds came, but often nothing seemed to be done. I have seen and heard those farmers, as they would meet and chat under the great trees before the morning service. Often they would talk about this and that and then one would say to the other: "Neighbor, have you any burden for souls today?" and the answer would come back rather shrinkingly: "No, neighbor, I haven't any special burden, yet, for souls, I am sorry to say." And the next day that would be repeated. They would thus talk around on the edges of the meeting, maybe for days, and then one would say: "Have you any burden about this meeting today? Have you any burden for souls today?" And the answer would be with trembling lip and with eyes suffused with tears: "I have, O neighbor, I have. God is my judge, how last night I felt to call upon Him through the long, long night, and I saw my own boys lost, and I saw your boys lost, and I saw our neighborhood lost. Oh, I have a burden for souls I cannot describe." I was at first too small to know what it all meant, but I can recall with what awe I would listen to it all, and even as a little child my soul was perfectly sure that God was somewhere near. And He was! And when we would go into the old country meeting house, on such a day, and the meeting would begin, and trembling lips would lead the prayers, and the hymns would be sung, God would come down into that meeting, and men that day were brought down by the life-giving Spirit of God. Whereas for days before the meetings were perfunctory and stilted and cold, now they were kindled into a strange glow. Sobs were heard on every side, and lost men asked: "What must we do to be saved?" What had happened, brethren? That "burden of souls" had come to God's people, without which soulwinning effort is largely in vain. Whenever they have that "burden of souls," things glorious always come to pass in the kingdom of God.

We had better wait: we had better betake ourselves to the quiet place; we had better search our hearts, and beg Him to search them for us; we had better go alone, each one for himself or herself, and talk with God, each one pouring out his soul to this effect: "O God, give me to feel about Your work like You wish. Come down in Your own way, and open the gates to my soul, so that I shall feel about Your work as You wish." You and I need to do that, brethren, and we need to do that tonight, with special reference to the work that is just now before us.

Some months ago a pastor was out in a vast country

camp meeting. A large arbor was provided, and from night to night there gathered a mighty crowd, so that the pastor needed to put his voice out to the last limit to be heard. But for days, so far as could be judged, nothing much was done. One night the preacher went to his room, and was making ready to retire, when the gentleman with whom he stopped came in. The host had very little to say, and the preacher made ready for sleep, and now was in the bed, while the host sat there on the cot on the other side of the room. Both slept in the same room. The good wife of the host was gone, having departed a few years before to be with the Lord. He had two grown daughters, popular and beautiful, but worldly—worldly, it seemed, after an unusual fashion. He sat over there that night on his cot, and after awhile, just as the preacher was ready to sleep, a sob was heard. The preacher looked up, and beheld his kindly friend with his face in his hands, and his great body fairly quivering. Said the preacher: "What is the trouble?" calling his host by name. He answered: "You ought to know what the trouble is. You have been in my home for three or four days. You ought to know what the trouble is." The preacher said: "Yes, I do; it is the girls." The host replied: "It is even so. Their mother is gone, and the sense of responsibility for them comes over me tonight as I never felt it before in all my life." Then he added: "Oh, if Mary (that was the older one) would only come to Christ, if she would only come to Christ, the problem, I think, would be settled with Jennie. Jennie always does what Mary does." The preacher said: "Well, we will pray for Mary tonight," and out of his bed he came, and knelt by his host. They talked to God about Mary, specifically about her, that the Almighty Savior might Himself take hold of her heart, and bring her to Himself. She was an amiable, beautiful girl, as has been said, but utterly indifferent about the claims of the soul, so far as could be seen. Then the preacher went back to his bed. After a while the door stood ajar, and the anxious father was seen quietly going out through the moonlight, and then the door was closed, and the preacher was soon asleep. In the early morning time the door was again quietly opened, and in came the host. A glance at his cot showed that he had been absent for the night. The preacher asked: "Where have you been?" And the answer was: "I will tell you about it, but you need not speak of it to the others. It is not a matter to be spoken of. I have been out there all night long talking to God about Mary; and that is not all. Mary will come to Christ today." Said the preacher: "Do you look for that?" He simply answered: "Yes, you will see that blessed result today." And that day, when the preacher finished his sermon at the morning meeting, and asked, while they sang, If anybody had found the Savior, to come and confess Him before all the people. Before they could start the music at all, Mary came with smiling face, and said: "I found Him while you preached." Do you doubt, my brethren, that there was a vital connection between that man's prayer and that child's return to Christ? The very next day, before the preacher had preached ten minutes, the other daughter, Jennie, rose up in the midst of the great crowd, and said: "Papa, I have found the Savior, too." I ask again, do you doubt that there was a vital connection between that prayer and that child's return to Christ? O God, burden us for souls! Burden us for souls! Ah, Paul had the "burden for souls." Hear him: "I say the truth in Christ, I lie not, my conscience also bearing me witness in the Holy Ghost, that I have great heaviness and continual sorrow in my heart. For I could wish that myself were accursed from Christ, for my brethren, my kinsmen, according to the flesh." The "burden for souls"—may God give it to us all! This is God's way—may His way be ours!

Why is this God's way? The reasons for it could be multiplied. Here are some. This is God's plan. Because in His own infinite wisdom He chose that it should be His plan, that is enough for us. God has revealed all along that one of the mightiest instruments in His kingdom for the furtherance of His cause in this world, for the turning of men to Christ, is prayer. See the injunctions to us to pray. We are to pray without ceasing. We are to pray for all men. We are not to so sin against the Lord, and so sin against men, as to cease praying for men. Behold how the

Scriptures magnify the place of prayer in the kingdom of God for the furtherance of His truth. It is God's plan, and we are to address ourselves to God's plan. Whenever we know God's mind about anything, then we have reached the end of the debate. We are to obey Him unreservedly.

And, then, we go further, and see that as labor is good for us in the world physical, so is it in the world spiritual. Spiritual labor is an exercise of incalculable moment. As in the physical world physical labor is for our upbuilding, in the world spiritual, spiritual labor, the exercising of ourselves to godliness, is the thing made very much of in the Scriptures.

Nor is that all. This kind of waiting upon God, this kind of confession of helplessness, and of supplication for grace and power, fits us to take care of people when they are saved. O brethren, how sad it is that our young Christians, so many times, get such a pitiful start in the Christian life! It is a great thing for a Christian to be well born, and that is one reason why we need to guard the churches of Jesus Christ. The churches of Jesus Christ are the supreme centers of evangelization. One of the things we have most earnestly to protest against, in these times, is the carrying away of evangelistic efforts from the churches of Jesus Christ. The churches are the hotbeds wherein the plants are to be grown to the Savior's honor. This is certainly a time when the churches need to give their most vigorous and faithful attention to this meaningful truth. Ring it out everywhere that the churches are the centers where evangelistic effort may be most wisely conducted. When Christ's church is spiritual, and calls upon Him with all humility, and with self-abnegation, and He answers back, and gives them a soul saved, then the church is ready to take care of that soul. Why is it that in very many of our churches vast numbers remain little spiritual babes all their lives? The answer is their start was bad. Their surroundings were not of a gracious sort. They were not put on the right track, and kept going on the right track. We are ready to take care of the young converts, when they come to us in answer to the right sort of prayer. What would become of that little new-born babe if it should be taken from its mother's arms, and thrown into the snow banks? And what will become of the little new-born child of God if it be ushered into a church where the atmosphere is lukewarm, and worldly, and indifferent to God's claims? There is likely to be one outcome, only, to that little religious life. The shipwreck of happiness and usefulness, for the most part. Our God has ordained this great method of carrying on His work, so that when souls are given to us, we are able to take care of them after the right fashion.

Not only that, but this is His plan, in order to teach us what we seem to forget most quickly of all—salvation is of the Lord. That is the truth that we seem to learn last of all, and the truth that we seem to forget most quickly of all—salvation is of the Lord. Oh, we accept it theoretically. You ask if we believe it, and with great promptness we answer that we do, and yet, do we? How much do we believe it? How long we are forgetting that vital truth, that we can raise men from that cemetery yonder as easily as we can regenerate the most amiable child in your Sunday school to God—that we can speak a world like this into life as easily as we can regenerate the most lovely soul in this city! Salvation is a divine work. Regeneration is a divine work. Conviction for sin is a divine work. The turning of men to God is a divine work. The making of men ready for heaven is a divine work. We learn that when we are on our knees before God. When we are out talking, and moving among men, we may go a great deal on the doctrine of salvation by works, but when we are on our faces before God, our helplessness is born in upon us, and then, with self-abnegation and a sense of our utter insufficiency, we humbly wait upon God for Him to do His work. And, mark it, when our attitude is right before Him, He always uses us to do His work.

Will we make this prayer in our text personal tonight? That is the crucial point I must ask you to face. Will we make this prayer of our text, tonight, personal? "Wilt thou not revive us again, that thy people here may rejoice in thee?" Will we make it personal? Do we wish for it to be personal? I am going to ask you that direct question, and

I am going to ask you to answer it, and I beseech you to answer it in sincerity and truth. Is this our prayer tonight? For let us know full well that each one of us shall be a helper or a hindrance in this proposed work. All along we are one of these two things in Christ's work. I speak now to Christians. I speak to those who have named Christ's name, who know and profess His cause to love. We are one of these two things in Christ's work. We are either helpers or hinderers in giving salvation to the perishing around us.

Who hinders Christ's work? First of all, the idle Christian hinders His work. Christians are not made to be idle. They are not made to be dumb. They are not made for their lips to be sealed so that they give forth no testimony to the dying around them. Christians are made to be busy. Christians are left in the world to be active, to be active for Jesus Christ. The idle Christian, then, hinders the cause of God in the earth. O Christian, if you are idle, you are hindering somewhere the advance of the great kingdom of God. The idleness of Christians surely hinders the march of the kingdom of God. Call to mind those solemn words of Jesus: "He that is not with me is against me; and he that gathereth not with me scattereth abroad." What does your heart say to that? Jesus cursed the fig tree because it was idle. It ought to have born fruit, and it did not, therefore He cursed it. Meroz of old was cursed because Meroz was idle. Meroz did not take up arms against the other tribes of Israel. Meroz did not lift up the black flag, and turn traitor to Israel. Meroz simply stayed at home and left her brothers to go out and fight the battle, and they went out and fought, and won, but with their victorious refrain there was mingled the refrain of the curse of the angel of God: "Curse ye Meroz, curse ye bitterly the inhabitants thereof; because they came not to the help of the Lord, to the help of the Lord against the mighty." The idle Christian hinders God's work.

Nor is that all. The Christian not right with God hinders His work, and this is a matter of unspeakable gravity, if only we rightly knew it. If he is not right in his outward conduct, we can see how that hinders God's work;

but, brethren, what wounds the Lord Jesus Christ receives in the house of His friends, His real friends, from men who do love Him, men who, if they were crowded to the wall, would die for Him! And yet what wounds He receives at the hands of such men, fall many a time, by their inconsistent words and their inconsistent works. How we hinder the cause of Jesus Christ ourselves! We need not trouble so much about the attacks of some blatant infidel out yonder, who rails against the Bible. That is not the supreme trouble at all, but the trouble supreme to the advancement of our Lord's kingdom in this world is with the people of His kingdom, with those who love it, and who are of it, and yet whose lives do not harmonize with it. There is our supreme trouble. If we are saying wrong things, or if we are doing wrong things; if, in our lives, inconsistencies may be seen; if there is marked worldliness, and if we fall so far short of the characteristics of what a Christian ought to have, so that men about us believe that our religion is just a theory, and not the dominating passion of our lives, then are we hindering the cause of Christ to a very sad degree.

Nor is that all. We hinder the cause of Christ, oh, so sadly, even though outwardly all may seem to be well with us, if inwardly it is not well with us. I do not know of any thought for the Christian more terribly serious than this—that the secret condition of his heart, which condition his wife does not know, cannot know—nor his most intimate earthly companion; which condition is known only to him and to God, the secret condition of his heart, is helping men in this city heavenward, or turning them hellward. The secret condition of your heart, a condition where no other eye can look, save One, that secret condition is now helping men up, or dragging them down, even as you sit in this building tonight. If a man's heart be right with God, then one prayer prayed from such a heart will have more power with God and with men than a thousand years of praying if the heart be all wrong with God. No wonder, then, that David prayed: "O God, restore unto me the joy of Thy salvation." Not salvation, mind you. He had that, but he prayed, "Give me back again the joy of Thy salvation, and then I will teach transgressors Thy ways, and then sinners shall be converted unto God." When a man is right with God, then there is power in his praying. When a man is right with God, he may lock the heavens, as did Elijah, or, like him, he may unlock them. Mind you, it is the supplication of a "righteous" man that avails much. So the secret condition of our hearts is helping now, or hindering now, these appointed gospel meetings, and will help or hinder them all along. If there is one picture in the Bible more than another that is solemn in the extreme, it is the picture of Achan's secret sin and the doom that followed in Joshua's army, in the olden time, which sin was known only to himself and to God, until Achan was searched and exposed. O brethren, I had this night rather be nailed up in my coffin and buried alive than to go through these gospel meetings with my heart all wrong, and my soul out of harmony with God; for I will either help or I will hinder others. Death were preferable infinitely than that a man should go on as a Christian, himself hindering salvation, himself hindering the blessed current of life that comes from God to man. Death were preferable to that. But every Christian is one of these two things—a hinderer or a helper. He is a channel through which God is pleased to send His grace and blessings to lost men, or he is a clog to stop up that channel.

Is this text our prayer tonight? "Revive us again"—do we pray it? Know this, dear friends, God has a blessing for us here, if—if what? God has a blessing for us here, blessed be His name, if only we wish it sufficiently. There is a recipe for soulwinning effort given back yonder in the seventh chapter of 2 Chronicles, the observance of which never fails: "If my people, which are called by my name, shall humble themselves, and pray, and seek my face, and turn from their wicked ways; then I will hear from heaven, and will forgive their sins, and will heal their land." Don't you see it? The observance of that recipe never fails, and never will. We shall have here a great blessing, brethren, if we will faithfully live out the truth of this one verse.

Are we going to be satisfied if Christ's people are not revived? Then they will not be. Are we going to be satisfied if men all about us are not convicted for sin and by divine power turned to Christ? Can we be satisfied if that result does not come? Then it will not come. Any preacher who can complacently preach on, month in and month out, and year in and year out, without seeing men converted; who can preach on through all that, and eat heartily and sleep soundly, will not see many converts under his ministry. I tell you, it is a life and death business in which we are engaged. Any church that can sit with folded hands and be satisfied if men are not turned to God, that can be easy with such a condition, will not have men added to her, whose testimony will be, "In that place I was turned to God." Do we wish to be revived? We shall have a great turning to God here, blessed be His name, if we wish it enough.

May I take one moment more just to talk to you about your plain duty? O God, bear You in upon us tonight the realization of this thought: We are left here to speak to dying men and women and children, at every possible place, and in every possible way, concerning the saving grace of Jesus Christ. Shall I talk to you about such duty? You Christians are to remember that teaching school is incidental; practicing medicine is incidental; pleading law is incidental; being a farmer is incidental. All these things are but mere incidents in the life that you are left here to live. The supreme thing for which you live is to point men to Christ. Shall I talk to you about your responsibility? That is indeed, a solemn question: "Am I my brother's keeper?" The answer must be that I am his keeper to the limit of my ability to help him. And by just letting him alone; by simple neglect, I may become my brother's spiritual murderer. Yonder is a man, let us suppose, dying on the streets of Dallas tonight. You will see him as you go home. He is sick, or drunk and helpless. We will imagine that it is a cold and stormy night. The snow and sleet are falling fast. The man is helpless. He lies in the gutter, all unconscious, it may be, of his awful danger. You look upon him, and pass him by. You must leave him to that awful fate, and in the morning he will be dead. And in the sight of heaven his blood will be required at your hands. You have no right to leave your brother to such a fate as that. Here is a neighbor or a child, a brother or a friend in spiritual night, and he does not realize it. He is condemned under the law of God, and he does not apprehend it. He may be in eternity tomorrow, and he does not take it to heart. He is without God, and without hope, and without light, and without life, and without grace, and without salvation, and you know it. Leaving him alone to die in his sins with such knowledge in your possession means that going down the dusty way of death his blood may be required at your hands.

Do you wish for God to revive you and this church and His people here just as He wishes to do it? Do you men and women here tonight wish Him to send you that quickening of conscience, that renewal of strength, that restoring of the joy of salvation, that will help you to do what He asks at your hands? Do you wish that? Do you wish a revival here, just like He wishes it? What say your hearts? Answer honestly, and we are ready to be dismissed. Every man and woman here who answers back from the heart, "Before God, I do, tonight, go on record, with His eye upon me, and in the sight of men, that I wish Him to come during these quiet meetings, and absolutely have His way with me and with these meetings," will now, in this solemn moment, quietly signify such a wish by standing.

The Ministry of a Transfigured Church

John Henry Jowett (1864–1923) was known as "the greatest preacher in the English-speaking world." Born in Yorkshire, England, he was ordained into the Congregational ministry. His second pastorate was at the famous Carr's Lane Church, Birmingham, where he followed the eminent Dr. Robert W. Dale. From 1911–18, he pastored the Fifth Avenue Presbyterian Church, New York City; and from 1918–23, he ministered at Westminster Chapel, London, succeeding G. Campbell Morgan. He wrote many books of devotional messages and sermons.

This sermon is from *Great Pulpit Masters: J. H. Jowett,* published in 1960 by Fleming H. Revell.

John Henry Jowett

6

THE MINISTRY OF A TRANSFIGURED CHURCH

> And when the day of Pentecost was come, they were all together in one place. And suddenly there came from heaven a sound as of the rushing of a mighty wind, and it filled all the house where they were sitting. And there appeared unto them tongues parting asunder, like as of fire: and it sat upon each one of them. And they were all filled with the Holy Spirit, and began to speak with other tongues, as the Spirit gave them utterance. . . . And when this sound was heard, the multitude came together! (Acts 2:1–4, 6).

THE WONDER INSIDE the church aroused inquisitive interest without. There came to the church an exceptional and plentiful endowment, and, as by the constraint of a mystic gravitation, the outside crowd began to move, like the waters swayed by the moon. The crowd may have moved toward the church in the temper of a flippant curiosity, or in the spirit of unfriendly revolt, or in the solemn mood of appropriating awe. Whatever may have been the constraint, the waters were no longer stagnant, the masses were no longer heedless and apathetic; the heedlessness was broken up, interest was begotten, and "the multitude came together."

Is the modern church the center of similar interest and wonder? Is there any awed and mesmeric rumor breathing through the streets, stirring the indifferent heart into eager questions? The modern church claims immediate kinship and direct and vital lineage with that primitive fellowship in the upper room. Does she manifest the power of the early church? Does she reveal the same magnetic influence and constraint?

I know that "the kingdom of God cometh not with observation." And so it is with the spring. The spring "cometh not with observation," but you speedily have tokens that

75

she is here. She can hide her coming behind March squalls, and she can step upon our shores in the rough attire of a blustering and tempestuous day; but even though her coming may be without observation, her presence cannot be hid. And even so it is with the kingdom: she may make no noisy and ostentatious display of her coming, but the sleeping seeds feel her approach, and the valley of bones experiences an awakening thrill, and "there is nothing hid from the heat thereof." I think, therefore, that we are justified in seriously inquiring as to the "resurrection power" of our churches, the measure of their quickening influence, their net result in reaching and stirring and consecrating the energies of a community. How do they stand in the judgment? Is the Pentecostal morning repeated, and is the gracious miracle the talk of the town? Does the multitude come together, "greatly wondering"?

Carry the inquisition to the regular and frequent fellowship of the church. So many times a week her members gather together in the upper room. What happens in the hallowed shrine? Are we held in solemn and enriching amazement at the awful doings? And when we come forth again, is there about us a mysterious impressiveness which arrests the multitude, and which sends abroad a spirit of questioning like a healthy contagion? Can we honestly say that by our ordinary services the feet of the heedless crowd are stayed, and that the people come together "greatly wondering"? In answer to all these searching questions I think that even the most optimistic of us will feel obliged to confess that the general tendency is undisturbed, that we do not generate force enough to stop the drift, and that the surrounding multitude remains uninfluenced.

Now, when we consider these unattracted or alienated peoples, we can roughly divide them into three primary classes. First, there are those who never think about us at all. So very remote are the highways of their thought and life that the impulse of the church is spent before it reaches their mental and moral abode. We can scarcely describe their attitude as one of indifference, because the mood of indifference would imply a negligent sense of our existence, and I can discern no signs of such perception. We contribute no thread to the fabric of their daily life. We bring no nutriment to the common meal; we do not even provide a condiment for the feast. Our presence in the city brings neither pleasure nor pain, neither sweet nor bitter, neither irritation nor ease; their souls are not disquieted within them, neither are they lulled into a deeper and more perilous sleep. We are neither irritants nor sedatives; to this particular class we simply do not exist.

And then, secondly, there are those who have thought about us, and as a result of their thinking have determined to ignore us. For all simple, positive, and progressive purposes we are no longer any good. We are exhausted batteries; we have no longer the power to ring a loud alarm, or to light a new road, or to energize some heavy and burdensome crusade. Our once stern and sacrificial warfare has now become a bloodless and self-indulgent quest. It is not only that the once potent shell cases have been emptied of their explosive content, they have been converted into dinner gongs! The once brilliant and unconditional ethical ideal has been dimmed and shadowed by worldly compromise. The pure and oxygenated flame of righteous passion has been changed into the fierce but smoky bonfire of sectarian zeal. We are looked upon as engaged in petty and childish controversy, losing ourselves in vague and nebulous phraseology, decking ourselves in vestures and postures as harmless and indifferent as the dresses worn at a fancy ball. That is the estimate formed of us by a vast section of the thinking crowd. You will find it reflected week by week in the labor papers, where we are regarded as straws in some side bay of a mighty river, riding serenely round and round and round, and we do not even show the drift of the stream, the dominant movement of our age. Our speech and our doings are of interest to the antiquary, but for all serious, practical, forceful, and aspiring life our churches do not count.

And, thirdly, there are those who think about us and who are constrained by their thinking into the fiercest and most determined opposition. To these men the church is not like Bunyan's "Giant Pope," alive but impotent, and "by reason of age, and also of the many shrewd brushes that he met with in his younger days, grown so crazy and stiff in his joints that he can do little more than sit in his cave's mouth, grinning at pilgrims as they go by, and biting his nails because he cannot come at them." No, to this class the church can do more than grin; it can reach and tear, and its ministry is still destructive. Its influence is perverse and perverting. Its very faith is a minister of mental and moral paralysis. Its dominant conceptions befog the common atmosphere, and chill and freeze "the genial currents of the soul." Its common postures and practices, its defenses and aggressions, perpetuate and confirm human alienations and divisions. The church cannot be ignored; it is not a harmless and picturesque ruin; it is a foul fungus souring the common soil, and for the sake of all sweet and beautiful things its nefarious influence must be destroyed.

This is by no means an exhaustive analysis of the alienated multitude, but it is sufficiently descriptive for my present purpose. In each of these three great primary classes the people stand aloof, indifferent and resentful, and the church is not endowed with that subduing and triumphant impressiveness which would turn their reverent feet toward herself. Now, how stands it with the church? Does she seem fitted to strike, and arrest, and silence, and allure the careless or suspicious multitudes? What is there unique and amazing about her? Her Lord has promised her a marvelous distinctiveness. She is to be "a glorious church, not having spot or wrinkle, or any such thing." "A glorious church," shining amid all the surrounding twilights with the radiance of a splendid noon! "Not having spot": no defect, no blemish, no impaired function, no diseased limb! "Or wrinkle": there shall be no sign of age about her, or any waste; she shall never become an anachronism; she shall always be as young as the present age, ever distinguished by her youthful brow, and by her fresh and almost boisterous optimism! "Or wrinkle, or any such thing." Mark the final, holy swagger of it, as though by a contemptuous wave of the hand the apostle indicates the entire rout of the unclean pests that invade and attack an apostate church. "Or any such thing"!

Are these great words of promise in any high degree descriptive of our own church? Is this our distinctiveness? "Not having spot": have we no withered hands, no halt, no blind, no lame, no lepers? "Or wrinkle": are we really distinguished by the invincible and contagious energies of perpetual youth? Does not the holding up of this great ideal throw our basal defects into dark and ugly relief? The pity of it all is just this, that the church, with all its loud and exuberant professions, is exceedingly like "the world." There is no clean, clear line of separation. In place of the promised glories we have a tolerable and unexciting dimness; in place of superlative whiteness we have an uninteresting gray; and in place of the spirit of an aggressive youthfulness we have a loitering and time-serving expediency. There would be no difficulty if only we had seized upon the fullness of our resources, and had become clothed with the riches of our promised inheritance, in men being able to distinguish, in any general company, the representatives of the church of the living God. There would be about them the pervasive joy of spiritual emancipation, resting upon all their speech and doings like sunlight on the hills. There would be about them a spiritual spring and buoyance which would enable them to move amid besetting obstacles with the nimbleness of a hart. "Thou hast made my feet like hinds' feet!" "By my God have I leaped over a wall!" There would be about them the fine serenity which is born of a mighty alliance. And there would be the strong, healthy pulse of a holy and hallowing purpose, beating in constant and forceful persistence. Such characteristics would distinguish any man, and any company, and any church, and the startled multitude would gather around in questioning curiosity. But the alluring wonder is largely absent from our church. Men pass from the world into our precincts as insensible of any difference as though they had passed from one side of the street to the other, and not feeling as though they had been transported from the hard, sterile glare of the city thoroughfare into the fascinating beauties of the Devonshire lane.

What, then, do we need? We need the return of the wonder, the arresting marvel of a transformed church, the phenomenon of a miraculous life. I speak not now of the wonders of spasmodic revivals; and, indeed, if I must be perfectly frank, my confidence in the efficient ministry of these elaborately engineered revivals has greatly waned. I will content myself with the expression of this most sober judgment, that the alienated and careless multitude is not impressed by the machinery and products of our modern revivals. The ordinary mission does not, and cannot, reach the stage at which this particular type of impressiveness becomes operative. The impressiveness does not attach to "decisions," but to resultant life. The wonder of the world is not excited by the phenomena of the penitent bench, but by what happens at the ordinary working-bench in the subsequent days. The world is not impressed by the calendar statement that at a precise particular moment winter relinquished her sovereignty to spring; the real interest is awakened by the irresistible tokens of the transition in garden, hedgerow, and field. It is not the new birth which initially arrests the world, but the new and glorified life. It is not, therefore, by spasmodic revivals, however grace-blessed they may be, that we shall excite the wonder of the multitude, but by the abiding miracle of a God-filled and glorious church. What we need, above all things, is the continuous marvel of an elevated church, "set on high" by the King, having her home "in the heavenly place in Christ," approaching all things "from above," and triumphantly resisting the subtle gravitation of the world, the flesh, and the Devil. It is not only multitudes of decisions that we want, but preeminently the heightening of the life of the saved, the glorification of the saints. The great Evangelical Revival began, not with the reclamation of the depraved, but with the enrichment of the redeemed. It was the members of the Holy Club, moving amid the solemnities of grace and sacred fellowship, who were lifted up into the superlative stages of the spiritual life, and who in that transition took a step as great and vital as the earlier step from sin to righteousness. Their life became a high and permanent miracle, and their subsequent ministry was miraculous. That is the most urgent necessity of our day, a church of the superlative order, immeasurable heightened and enriched—a church with wings as well as feet, her dimness changed into radiance, her stammering changed into boldness, and presenting to the world the spectacle of a permanent marvel, which will fascinate and allure the inquiring multitude drawn together "not that they might see Jesus only, but Lazarus' also whom he has raised from the dead."

Now, what is the explanation of the comparative poverty and impotence of our corporate life? Why is the church not laden with the impressive dignities of her destined inheritance? Look at the manner of our fellowship. Is it such as to give promise of power and wealth? When we meet together, in worshiping communities, do we look like men and women who are preparing to move amid the amazing and enriching sanctities of the Almighty? Take our very mode of entry. It is possible to lose a thing by the way we approach it. I have seen a body of flippant tourists on the Rigi at the dawn, and by their noisy irreverence they missed the very glory they had come to see. "When ye come to appear before me, who hath required this at your hands, to trample my courts?" That loud and irreverent tramp is far too obtrusive in our communion. We are not sufficiently possessed by that spirit of reverence which is the "open sesame" into the realms of light and grace. We are not subdued into the receptiveness of awe. No, it is frequently asserted that in our day awe is an undesirable temper, a relic of an obsolete stage, a remnant of pagan darkness, a fearful bird of a past night, altogether a belated anachronism in the full, sweet light of the evangel of grace. I remember receiving a firm, but very courteous remonstrance from one of the children of light, because on the very threshold of a lovely summer's morning I had announced the hymn:

> Lo! God is here: let us adore
> And own how dreadful is this place.

And my friend said it was like going back to the cold, gray dawn, when disturbed spirits were speeding to their rest!

It was like moving amid the shadows and specters of Genesis, and he wanted to lie and bask in the calm, sunny noon of the Gospel by John! I think his letter was representative of a common and familiar mood of our time. I have no desire to return to the chill, uncertain hours of the early morning, but I am concerned that we should learn and acquire the only receptive attitude in the presence of our glorious noon. It is certain that many of the popular hymns of our day are very far removed from the hymn to which I have just referred. It is not that these hymns are essentially false, but that they are so one-sided as to throw the truth into disproportion, and so they impair and impoverish our spiritual life.

Here is one of the more popular hymns of our time:

> O that will be glory for me,
> When by His grace I shall look on His face,
> That will be glory, be glory for me!

Well, we all want to share in the inspiration of the great expectancy! It is a light and lilting song, with very nimble feet: but lest our thought should fashion itself after the style of these tripping strains, we need to hear behind the lilt "the voice of the great Eternal," sobering our very exuberance into deep and awful joy. "When by His grace I shall look on His face!" That is one aspect of the great outlook, and only one, and therefore incomplete. I find the complementary aspect in these familiar words, "With twain he covered his face!" That is quite another outlook, and it introduces the deepening ministry of awe, which I am afraid is so foreign to the modern mind. "I feel like singing all the day!" So runs another of our popular hymns. That would have been a congenial song for my friend on that radiant summer morning when his thoughtless minister led him up to the awful splendors of the great white throne! "I feel like singing all the day," and the words suggest that this ought to be the normal mood for all pilgrims on the heavenly way. I am not so sure about that, and I certainly have grave doubts as to whether the man who feels "like singing all the day" will make the best soldier when it comes to "marching as to war." "The

Lord is in his holy temple: let all the earth keep silence before him." That is a contemplation which seeks expression in something deeper than song. "There was silence in heaven about the space of half an hour." What had they seen, what had they heard, what further visions of glory had been unveiled, that speech and song were hushed, and the soul sought fitting refuge in an awe-inspired silence?

When I listen to our loud and irreverent tramp, when I listen to so many of our awe-less hymns and prayers, I cannot but ask whether we have lost those elements from our contemplation which are fitted to subdue the soul into silence, and to deprive it of the clumsy expedient of speech. We leave our places of worship, and no deep and inexpressible wonder sits upon our faces. We can sing these lilting melodies, and when we go out into the streets our faces are one with the faces of those who have left the theaters and the music halls. There is nothing about us to suggest that we have been looking at anything stupendous and overwhelming. Far back in my boyhood I remember an old saint telling me that after some services he liked to make his way home alone, by quiet byways, so that the hush of the Almighty might remain on his awed and prostrate soul. That is the element we are losing, and its loss is one of the measures of our poverty, and the primary secret of our inefficient life and service. And what is the explanation of the loss? Preeminently our impoverished conception of God. The popular God is not great, and will not create a great race. The church must not expect to strike humanity with startling and persistent impact if she carries in her own mind and heart the enfeebling image of a mean Divinity. Men who are possessed by a powerful God can never themselves be impotent. But have we not robbed the Almighty of much of His awful glory, and to that extent are we not ourselves despoiled? We have contemplated the beauties of the rainbow, but we have overlooked the dim severities of the throne. We have toyed with the light, but we have forgotten the lightning. We have rejoiced in the Fatherhood of our God, but too frequently the Fatherhood we have proclaimed has been throneless and effeminate. We have picked and chosen according to the weakness of our own tastes, and not according to the full-orbed revelation of the truth, and we have selected the picturesque and rejected the appalling. "And he had in his right hand seven stars"—yes, we can accept that delicate suggestion of encircling love and care! "And his countenance was as the sun shineth in his strength"—yes, we can bask in the distributed splendor of the sunny morn! "And out of his mouth went a sharp two-edged sword!"—and is that too in our selection, or has our cherished image been deprived of the sword? Why leave out that sword? Does its absence make us more thoughtful and braver men, or does it tend to lull us into an easefulness which removes us far away from the man who when he saw Him, "fell at his feet as dead"?

This mild, enervating air of our modern Lutheranism needs to be impregnated with something of the bracing salts of Calvinism. Our very Evangelicalism would be all the sturdier by the addition of a little "baptized Stoicism." Our water has become too soft, and it will no longer make bone for a race of giants. Our Lutheranism has been diluted and weakened by the expulsion of some of the sterner motive-elements which it possessed at its source. If we banish the conceptions which inspire awe, we of necessity devitalize the very doctrines of grace, and if grace is emasculated then faith becomes anemic, and we take away the very tang and pang from the sense of sin. All the great epistles of the Apostle Paul being in the awe-inspiring heights of towering mountain country, and all through the changing applications of the thought these cloud-capped eminences are ever in sight. Paul's eyes were always lifted up "unto the hills," and therefore his soul was always on its knees. If he rejoiced, it was "with trembling"; if he served the Lord, it was "with fear"; if he was "perfecting holiness," it was gain "in the fear of the Lord!" Always, I say, this man's eyes were upon the awful, humbling, and yet inspiring heights of revealed truth. Our modern theological country is too flat; there are not enough cool, unlifted snow-white heights—heights like Lebanon, to which the peasant can turn his feverish eyes even when he is engaged in the labors of the sweltering vale. "Wilt thou forsake the snows of Lebanon?" "His righteousness is like the great mountains!" "Go! stand on the mount before the Lord!" "In the year King Uzziah died I saw the Lord, high and lifted up!" "Holy, holy, holy is the Lord." That was a mountain view. "And I said, Woe is me!" And that was the consequent awe. If the ministers of the church were to swell in those vast uplifted solitudes strange things would happen to us. Our speech would be deepened in content and tone, and we should speak as they say John Fletcher of Madeley used to speak, "like one who had just left the immediate converse of God and angels." But not only so, there would be added to our speech the awful energy of a still more powerful silence. "Every year makes me tremble," said Bishop Westcott toward the end of his years—"every year makes me tremble at the daring with which people speak of spiritual things." Is not the good Bishop's trembling justified?

Some time ago I preached a sermon on the bitter cup which was drunk by our Lord and Savior Jesus Christ. I noticed that one of the papers, in a reference to the sermon, said that I had spoken on the sufferings of Christ "with charming effect." The words sent me to my knees in humiliation and fear. Soul of mine, what had I said, or what had I left unsaid, or through what perverting medium had I been interpreted? For the flippancy can be in the reporter as well as in the preacher, it can be in the religious press as well as in the consecrated minister. But let the application stand to me alone and let me once again remind myself of Westcott's trembling "at the daring with which people speak of spiritual things." Aye, we are reckless and therefore forceless in our speech: we are not mighty in our silences. There are some things which our people must infer from our reverent silences, things which can never be told in speech, and these mountain experiences are among them. That awe of the heights will deepen and enlarge both the ministry and the church, it will enrich both her speech and her silences, and it will make her character unspeakably masculine, forceful, and impressive. "If in any part of Europe a man was required to be burned, or broken on the wheel, that man was at Geneva, ready to depart, giving thanks to God, and singing psalms to Him." A mighty God makes irresistible men. History has proved, and experience confirms it today, that this mountain-thinking, with all its subduing austerities and shadows, would create a powerful and athletic church; a church of most masculine temper, courageous both in its aggressions and in its restraints, both in its confessions and its reserves, a church that would rouse and impress the world by the decisive vigor of its daily life—never dull, never feeble, but always and everywhere "fair as the moon, clear as the sun, and terrible as an army with banners." "O Zion, get thee up into the high mountains!"

But our impoverished conception of God is not the only cause of our comparative poverty and enfeeblement. The life of the church is expressed in two relationships, the human and the Divine. The Divine fellowship has been impoverished by lack of height; the human fellowship has been impoverished by lack of breadth. We have not drunk the iron water from the heart of the mountains, and we have therefore lacked a healthy robustness; we have not accumulated the manifold treasures of the far-stretching plain, and we have therefore lacked a wealthy variety. Our fellowship with God has been mean; our fellowship with man has been scanty. No, would it not be just the truth to say that the human aspects of our church fellowship suggest a treasure-house which has never been unlocked? The church is poor because much of her treasure is imprisoned; but she herself carries the liberating key to the iron gate! Our riches are buried in the isolated lives of individual members instead of all being pooled for the endowment of the whole fraternity. A very large part of the ample ministry of the κοινωία has been atrophied, if indeed it has ever been well sustained. I gratefully recognize the mystic, silent fellowship among the consecrated members of the church of Christ. I know that out of the very heart of "him that believeth" there inevitably flow "rivers of living water," and I delight to allow my imagination to rest upon the well irrigated country of this sanctified society. There is a mystic commerce altogether independent of human expedient or arrangement. We cannot bow together without some exchange of heavenly merchandise, without angel ministries carrying from island to island the unique and peculiar products of their climes. The rich and enriching history of the Society of Friends is altogether corroborative of this great truth of spiritual experience. "When I came into the silent assemblies of God's people," says Robert Barclay, "I felt a sweet power among them which touched my heart, and as I gave way to it, I found the evil weakening in me and the good raised up."

But the human side of the apostolic κοινωία includes riches other than these. It is not only a mystic interchange in the awful depths of the spirit; it is a fellowship of intelligence, it is a community of experience, it is the socializing of the individual testimony and witness. It is not only the subtle carriage of spiritual energy, it is the transference of visions, the sharing of discoveries, the assemblage of many judgments, whether in the hour of triumph or of defeat. "When ye come together, every one of you hath a psalm, hath a doctrine, hath a tongue, hath a revelation, hath an interpretation." That is the broader fellowship we lack, and we are all the poorer for it. The psalm that is born in one heart remains unsung, and the sadness it was fitted to remove from the heart of another abides like a clammy mist. The revelation that dawned upon one wondering soul is never shared, and so another remains in the cold imprisonment of the darkness. The private interpretation is never given, and for want of the key, many obstructing doors are never unlocked.

This is the neglected side of the apostolic fellowship, and for the want of it the church goes out to confront the world in the poverty of a starved individualism rather than in the rich and full-blooded vigor of her communistic strength. We are not realizing the social basis of the church's life; Christian fellowship comprehends not only a meeting at a common altar, but a meeting at a family hearth, for the reverent and familiar interchange of our experiences with God, and of what has happened to us in our warfare with the world, the flesh, and the Devil. In lieu of the broader and richer fellowship we have exalted the ministry of one man, and out of the limited pool of his experience—and sometimes they are not even experiences, but only fond and desirable assumption—the whole community has to drink, while the rest of the many pools remain untapped. And, oh, the treasures that are hidden in these unshared and unrevealed experiences! What have our matured saints to tell us of the things we wish to know? How did they escape the snare, or by what subtlety were they fatally beguiled? How did they take the hill, and where did they discover the springs of refreshing? What did they find to be the best footgear when the gradient was steep, and how did they comfort their hearts when they dug the grave by the way? And what is it like to grow old, and what delicacies does the Lord of the road provide for aged pilgrims, and have they seen any particular and wonderful stars in their evening sky? Are not all of us unspeakably poorer because these counsels and inspirations are untold? And our younger communicants— how are they faring on the new and arduous road? What unsuspected difficulties are they meeting? And what unsuspected provisions have they received? And what privilege of service has been given them, and what inspiring vision have they found in the task? And what have our stalwart warriors to tell us? How goes the fight in the business fields, on market and exchange? And what hidden secret has the Lord of light been unveiling to the ordained layman? What wealth of truth and glory? I say, these are breadths of the κοινωία we do not traverse, these are mines we do not work, and the output of our moral and spiritual energy is consequently small.

I know the perils which abound in these particular regions of exercised communion. Those who have the least to say may be readiest to speak. The spiritually insolvent may rise and talk like spiritual millionaires. The bloom of a delicate reserve may be destroyed, and flippant witnessing may become a substitute for deep experience. Easy familiarity may be made the standard of spiritual attainment, and sensational statements may be engendered by the hotbed of vanity and pride. In a fellowship meeting some members may speak from a subtle love of applause, while others may speak from an equally illicit sense of shame. I know all this, but I know also that there is nothing in the entire round of Christian worship and communion which is not exposed to abomination and abuse. There is not a single plant in your garden which is not the gathering ground of some particular pest; aye, and the more delicate and tender the plant, the more multitudinous are the foes. But you do not banish the plant because of the pests; you accept the plant and guard against the pests; and I for one think it not impossible to cultivate this larger, richer, more social and familiar fellowship, and at the same time to create an atmosphere in which these invasive perils shall be unable to breathe. Under God, everything depends upon your leader; and under God, cannot wise leaders be grown-leaders who shall be able, with a rare delicacy of tact born of deep and unceasing communion with God, to draw out the individual gift of witness and experience, and by the accumulated treasure to enrich the entire church? Our church is comparatively poor and unimpressive; here is a storehouse of untouched resources which I am convinced would immeasurably enrich and strengthen our equipment in our combined attack against the powers of darkness. We need to get higher up the mountains. And we need, too, to get farther out upon the plains. "O, for a closer walk with God!" And, "O, for a closer walk with man!" Closer to the great and holy God, that we may be possessed by a deepening and fertilizing awe; and closer to our brother, that we may move in the manifold inspiration and comfort of "mutual faith" and experience.

I have not been concerned with the suggestion of new expedients. It has not been my purpose to advocate or defend aggressive and unfamiliar enterprises. My eyes have not been upon the church's conduct, but upon her character; not upon her prospectus, but upon her capital; not upon her plan of campaign, but upon her fighting strength. "Like a mighty army moves the church of God!"

Yes, but does she? Are not her regiments sometimes almost Falstaffian in their bedraggled impotence? How shall she increase her fighting power? How shall she enrich her spirit of discipline? And I have answered: By taking thought of the untrodden heights and the untrodden breadths within her own circle, by claiming her purposed and buried resources in humanity and in God. I am convinced that in these ways we should make undreamed-of additions to the energy and impact of the church's strength. No church can walk along these unfrequented paths without acquiring the moments of sacrificial grace; and when the power of the church becomes awful and sacrificial, when she bears in her body the red "marks of the Lord Jesus," when there is "blood upon the lintel and the two side posts" of her door, you may be assured that the arrested multitude will come together, drawn by the mesmeric gravitation of her own irresistible strength. And not only strong shall the church become, strong in unselfish daring and persistence, but because of the very robustness of her strength she shall be tender with an exquisitely delicate compassion. I have yielded to none in the advocacy of "the wooing note" in the ministry of the Word, and with a growing and richer confidence I advocate it still. But there is the wooing note of a silly, simpering sentimentalism, and there is the wooing note of strong and masculine men who have been cradled and molded and homed in the austere nursery and school of the mountains. And where can you make your fine wooers if not among the deepening ministries of the mountains? "How beautiful upon the mountains are the feet of them that bring glad tidings!" I shall have no fear about the strength and sweetness of the wooing note when we are all the children of the heights.

Given these conditions, and I believe the church will move among the alienated multitudes with an illumined and fascinating constraint. The alienation of the people is not fundamental and ultimate. Deep down, beneath all the visible severances, there are living chords of kinship, ready to thrill and to respond to the royal note. Those living chords—buried, if you will, beneath the dead and deadening crust of formality and sin, buried, but buried alive—are to be found in Belgravia, where Henry Drummond, that man of the high mountains and the broad plains, awoke them to response by the strong, tender impact of a great evangel and a great experience. And those living chords are also to be found at the pit's mouth, among the crooked and pathetic miners, and they become vibrant with responsive devotion, as Keir Hardie has told us that his became vibrant, in answer to the awakening sweep of the strong, tender hands of the Nazarene. The multitude is not sick of Jesus; it is only sick of His feeble and bloodless representatives. When once again a great church appears, a church with the Lord's name in her forehead, a church with fine muscular limbs and face seamed with the marks of sacrifice, the multitude will turn their feet to the way of God's commandments. I sat a little while ago in one of the chambers of the National Gallery, and my attention was caught by the vast miscellaneous crowd as it sauntered and galloped through the rooms. All sorts and conditions of people passed by—rich and poor, the well-dressed and the beggarly, students and artisans, soldiers and sailors, maidens just out of school and women bowed and wrinkled in age. But, whoever they were, and however unarresting may have been all the other pictures in the chamber, every single soul in that mortal crowd stopped dead and silent before a picture of our Savior bearing His cross to the hill. And when the church is seen to be His body—His very body: His lips, His eyes, His ears, His hands, His feet, His brain, His heart, His very body—and when the church repeats, in this her corporate life, the brave and manifold doings of Judea and Galilee, she too shall awe the multitude, and by God's grace she shall convert the pregnant wonder into deep and grateful devotion.

Our times are disturbed, and hopefully and fruitfully disturbed, by vast and stupendous problems. On every side the latch is lifting, and the door of opportunity stands ajar. But we shall fail in our day, as other men have failed in their day, unless by faith and experience we enter into "the fellowship of his sufferings," and become clothed with "the power of his resurrection." Sound social economics are not enough; sound political principles are not enough; sound creeds and politics are not enough. The most robust and muscular principle will faint and grow weary unless it is allied with character which is rendered unique and irresistible by unbroken communion with the mind and will of God. It is "Christ in us" which is "the hope of glory," both for the individual and the State.

Let us abide in Him in total and glorious self-abandonment. Let nothing move us from our rootage. Let us "pray without ceasing," and let our consecration be so complete and confident that there may be presented to the world a church "alive unto God"; a church as abounding in signs of vitality as hedgerows in the spring; a church quickened in moral vision, in intellectual perception, in emotional discernment; a church acute, compassionate and daring, moving amid the changing circumstances of men in the very spirit of her Lord, and presenting everywhere the arresting ministry of "a hiding-place from the wind, a covert from the tempest, rivers of water in a dry place, and the shadow of a great rock in a weary land!"

NOTES

The Revival of Religion

Joseph Parker (1830–1902) was one of England's most popular preachers. Largely self-educated, Parker had pulpit gifts that soon moved him into leadership among the Congregationalists. He was a fearless and imaginative preacher who attracted both common people and the aristocracy, and he was particularly a "man's preacher." His *People's Bible* is a collection of the shorthand reports of the sermons and prayers Parker delivered as he preached through the entire Bible in seven years (1884–91). He pastored the Poultry Church, London, later called the City Temple, from 1869 until his death.

   This sermon is taken from Volume 12 of *The People's Bible* (London: Hazell, Watson and Viney, 1900).

Joseph Parker

7

THE REVIVAL OF RELIGION

Wilt thou not revive us again: that thy people may rejoice in thee? (Psalm 85:6).

IT IS WELL KNOWN that many Christians have come to have a distaste for the word "revival" when used with reference to religious work. To some extent I share that distaste. There has been so much exaggeration, so much fanatical excitement, and so much transient profession, that we cannot wonder at the revulsion which many sober-minded Christians feel when they hear the very word "revival." We believe that all got-up revivals are bad. You cannot organize a true revival; we cannot treat spiritual influences as fixed quantities; as the wind blows where it lists, so, often, is that sudden, profound, and irresistible impulse which rouses the church, and breaks in beneficently upon the deadly slumber and delusive security of the world. As a matter of fact, there have been extraordinary visitations of divine influence; there have been seasons when the Holy Spirit has made the earthquake, the fire, the rending wind, and the stormy tempest His ministers, and when men have been shaken with a wholesome fear, not knowing the way, yet feeling the nearness of the Lord. There have been great birthdays in the church, days on which thousands have been crucified with Jesus Christ, and multitudes have begun to sing loudly and lovingly His praise. There have been days of high festival in the sanctuary, when the silver trumpets have sounded, when prodigals have come back to sonship, when shepherds have returned with recovered flocks, when women have found the piece that was lost, and the dead have risen to immortal life. There have, too, been times when the people have realized with special vividness the personality and life-giving power of the Holy Spirit; when they have had the keys of interpretation wherewith to unlock the boundless treasures of the divine Word; when prayer was as the speech of love that never wearies; when the Sabbath shed its sacred glory over all the days of the week; when God's house shone with heavenly luster, and all life throbbed in joyful harmony with the purposes of God. We refer to these things as to matters of fact, and in doing so we wish to know whether such delights cannot be more permanently secured. At the same time let it be clearly said that we could not bear the strain of an ecstatic life; we are not constituted for constant rapture; we have to contend with the deceitfulness of the flesh; we have to fight and suffer upon the earth when the spirit would gladly escape on the wings of the morning to untroubled and hallowed scenes. Still, there is danger in supposing that because we cannot always live at the highest point of spiritual enthusiasm, we may be content with low attainments, or with a neutrality which attracts no attention to itself. Now there is something between the flame of a blazing ecstasy and the gray ashes of a formal profession; there is a steady and penetrating glow of piety, there is a fervor of love, there is an animated intelligence, a zealous affection, a godly yearning for personal progress and social evangelization, which, when found together, make up a life of delight in God and blessed service for men. To promote this realization we offer a few suggestions of whose value you can quickly form a sound opinion.

First of all, we are more and more assured that, as individual Christians, and as churches of Jesus Christ, we need to be very clear in our doctrinal foundations. Do let us get a distinct idea of the principal points in the Christian faith. Beginning with the doctrine of sin, let us strive after God's view of it. To Him sin is infinitely hateful; He cannot tolerate it with the least degree of allowance; it troubles His otherwise perfect and happy universe; it despoils human nature; it overthrows all that is divine in manhood; it calls into existence the worm that gnaws forever; it is the cause of death and the source of hell. To underestimate the heinousness of sin is to put ourselves out of the line of God's view; to understand sin is to understand redemption. Sin interprets the Cross; sin shows what is meant by God's love. Have we, as individuals and churches, lost the true notion of sin? Is it no longer infinitely abominable to us? Is it toned down to something almost indistinguishable? We cannot be right in our relation to Jesus Christ, we cannot be just to His holy Cross, until we regard sin with unutterable repugnance, until we rise against it in fiery indignation, fighting it with all the energy of wounded love, and bringing upon it the condemnation of concentrated and implacable anger. We are not speaking of what are called great sins; nor thinking of murder, of commercial plunder, of adultery, drunkenness, or theft; we are speaking of sin as sin, sin nestling secretly in the heart, sin rolled under the tongue as a sweet morsel, sin indulged in secret places, sin perverting the thought, sin poisoning the love, sin sucking out the lifeblood of the soul; thinking of sin, not of sins—of the fact, not of the details; we ask, with passionate yet well-considered pointedness, Have we not been led to underestimate the guilt of sin?

Out of a true knowledge of sin will come a true appreciation of Jesus Christ as the Savior. Apart from this, He will be a strange teacher; with it, He will be the Redeemer for whom our hearts have unconsciously longed when they have felt the soreness and agony of sin. We could sum up the Christian creed in a sentence, yet that sentence contains more than all the libraries in the world. The short but all-including creed—the faith which bears us up above all temptation and all controversy, the faith in which we destroy the power of the world, and soar into the brightness of eternal day—is this: I believe in Jesus Christ, the Son of God! The heart hungers for Him, our sin cries out for His mercy, our sorrow yearns for His coming, and when He does come He speaks just the word that the soul needs; He understands us; He knows us altogether; He can get down into the low, dark pit into which sin has thrown us; He draws us to His Cross; He hides our sins in His sacrifice; He shows us how God can be honored, yet the sinner forgiven; He destroys the Devil, and puts within us the Holy Spirit; He so fills us with life that death has no longer any terror with which to affright us. I believe in Jesus Christ, the Son of God; His word is the best witness of its own power; it touches life at every point; it is most precious when most needed; it goes into our business, and lays down the golden rule; it follows us in our wanderings, and bids us return; it is always pure, noble, unselfish, unworldly; it gives us a staff for the journey, a sword for the battle, a shelter from the storm, and in the last darkening hour it gives us the triumph of immortality. This is the witness of ten thousand times ten thousand histories. We do not wonder at worldly or dead-hearted men calling this declamation: to them it is declamation; to them, indeed, it is madness; yet can we, who have known what it is to have Christ coming to us through all our sin, say of a truth that, when we are most mad, we are most wise—the ecstasy of love is the reason of faith.

If we lay firmly hold of these two points—that is, the sinfulness of sin, and the work of Jesus Christ—we shall come to know what is meant by what we have ventured to call the glow of piety. Only the liberated slave can know the joy of freedom—only the recovered leper can appreciate fully the blessing of health. Let an emancipated slave tell of the joys of liberty, and the man who has never felt the grip of a shackle will at once pronounce him a declaimer; let a recovered leper say all he can of the delights of health, and the man who has never known a day's sickness will probably think him more or less of a fool. It is so with our preaching, or with our true Christian living; it is not set in the common key of the world; it cannot be judged by the rules of carnal criticism; when it is praised as regular, thoughtful, prudent, let us beware, lest under these flattering names be hidden a deep, yet almost unconscious apostasy. By these strong words we seek to point out as the only solid basis of a genuine revival of religion the need of being distinct and positive in our faith. Let us know what we believe. Let us be able to say with sureness and thankfulness what is the Rock on which we stand.

Do not say that this is clipping the wings of mental freedom; do not charge me with narrowness or sectarianism; only be on the Rock, and you shall have upward scope enough; only be sure about Jesus Christ as at once the Interpreter of sin, and the Savior of sinners, and you may fly far on the wings of fancy; you may bring gems from many a mine, and flowers from many a garden. You may have your own way of saying things, you may speculate, and suggest, and discuss, only never turn sin into a flippant riddle, and never set up the Savior as a mere conundrum in theology. Are we thoroughly at one on these two points? Do we know sin in its essential, unchangeable loathsomeness? Do we love Jesus Christ as the only, the Almighty, and the ever-blessed Savior? Then, out of this should come an intense fervor of piety. We should have strength here; we should come back to these points from all the wanderings of fancy, and all the bewilderments of temptation; we should hasten to these doctrines when the anxieties of religious thought are heavy upon us; we should publish these doctrines in explanation and defense of an enthusiasm which must appear as madness to those who have not seen the unseen or felt the power of an endless life. To have one strong point of faith is of more consequence than to enjoy the most splendid speculations, which vanish like an enchanted dream when touched by the realities of sorrow and death. To the young and ardent let me particularly, and with most anxious love, give a word of caution. There are not wanting men who will tell you that it is of little or no consequence what you believe. To the young mind this is very pleasant: it saves trouble, it leaves conscience untouched, it looks like liberty. Let me speak strongly yet soberly about this teaching. Having examined it, seen its effects on many men, and watched its general results, I am prepared to characterize it as a lie. I do not hesitate to teach that faith is the very root of life. What a man most deeply believes, that he most truly is. All earnest life is but a working out of earnest conviction. No man can live a deep, true, great life who lives upon the chances of the day, without convictions, without purposes, without principles on which he is prepared to risk the whole issue and destiny of his life. You will, after all, leave much unsettled; you will not encroach one iota upon the liberty of any man; you will still hold your mind open to receive new impressions, new visions of truth, new aspects of duty; yet you will have no standing place, no home, no rest, until you can say with the love and fire of your heart, I believe in Jesus Christ, the Son of God.

In the next place, having a distinct idea of what we truly believe, we must have a public ministry which is faithful to the spirit and demands of Jesus Christ. We would speak with great caution upon this point, so far as personal methods of ministry are concerned. Every man must preach in the way that to him is best, most powerful, and most useful. What we wish to say is, that all Christian ministers are called to be faithful to Jesus Christ in seeking the salvation of men. In my view of ministerial life, there is too much attention paid in the pulpit to controversial subjects. We have a great positive work to do. We have affirmative truths to teach. We have to cast out devils, not by controversy, but by divinely-revealed and authoritative truths. If we wish to take our part in the controversies of the world, the press is at our service; in the pulpit let us preach the kingdom of our Lord Jesus Christ, and mightily plead with men to repent and believe the Gospel. There is scope enough for all our powers. We shall have to acquaint ourselves deeply with human nature; we shall have to read the heart until we know its devices, imaginations, and cunning deceits; we shall have to study the power of sin in the soul; we shall have to suffer with Jesus Christ; we shall have to inquire diligently into God's righteousness, mercy, and love; night and day we shall have to study the mystery of Redemption, and in doing all these things our every power will be absorbed and exhausted. If now and again, specially for the benefit of young men, we may have occasion to refer to controversies, let the reference be made with the lofty earnestness of men who are intent upon the salvation of those who hear us. We must not throw off the old words—Repentance, Faith, Salvation; and the things that they signify must be the very life-blood of our ministry. In any genuine revival of interest in Christianity there must be a revived interest in a preached Gospel. The sanctuary will be thronged, and the thronging listeners will be justly impatient of everything that does not bear immediately and intensely upon the salvation of men. We sometimes talk of adapting our preaching to the age in which we live, of keeping it abreast with contemporary culture, and addressing ourselves to the habits of men of taste. In all this there may be truth enough barely to save it from the charge of insanity. My deepening impression is that, however we may modify our manner, the doctrine which is adapted to all ages, to all tastes, to all circumstances, is that Jesus Christ came into the world to save sinners. Then must we be made to feel that the doctrines of the Gospel are humbling doctrines; that they smite down our natural pride and self-trustfulness, that they kill before they make alive that out of our utter impoverishment and nothingness they bring all that is distinctive and enduring in Christian manhood. Black will be the day, disastrous the hour, in which the Gospel is pared down to meet the notions of any men. The Gospel is less than nothing, if it be not the grandest revelation of the heart of God to the heart of man; and being a revelation, it must of necessity be clothed with an authority peculiarly emphatic and decisive. We believe the Gospel to be God's answer to human sin and human sorrow; and if any man ask where is its authority, we answer, "The blind do see, the deaf hear, the dumb speak, the lame walk, the lepers cleansed, and the dead are raised to life." Christian living is the best explanation of Christian believing; Christianity is the best explanation of Christianity; and more preaching is the best answer to all opposition.

While there should be full and bold proclamation of evangelical doctrine in the pulpit, there should also be a system of teaching proceeding more privately. We believe thoroughly in sound, critical, extensive teaching. Some men have a peculiar gift in biblical teaching; those men should be encouraged to pursue their laborious but most necessary vocation. The preacher and teacher should be fellow-laborers. The preacher should collect men into great companies, arrest their attention by earnest and convincing statements of Christian truth, and then pass them on, so to speak, to the critical and patient teacher.

Thus the man of God will become thoroughly furnished—having received deep instruction, he will be able to give a reason for the faith and hope that are in him, and he will be strong to resist the importunities of those who are driven about by every wind of doctrine. We have had unjust and unreasonable expectations respecting the ministry. We have looked for all sorts of work from ministers; they have been expected to be eloquent preachers, popular lecturers, learned writers, acceptable visitors, skilled controversialists, untiring evangelists, and many other important and influential characters. This is the covetousness that tends to poverty. Let a man be one thing, and let him excel in it. I wish the Christian pulpit to be my world; in it I would work as a willing servant, and in it I would die like a soldier sword in hand. Another brother is a teacher, learned, critical, and patient with slow scholars; another is blessed with a high pastoral gift, by which he can make himself as an angel of God in the family; another is a ready writer, who can fascinate the eye of taste, or convince the stubborn-minded: be it so; it is right, it is best. When Christian truth and Christian feeling revive among us, we shall be as the heart of one man, each magnifying God in the other. We shall all be wanted; the trumpet, the flute, the organ, the stringed instrument—the soldier, the physician, the teacher—the orator, the scholar, the poet—the strong man, the gentle woman, the tender child—all will be wanted; and the only strife among us will be who can do most and do it best for the Lamb that was slain!

We have heard of a great musical composer who was conducting a rehearsal by four thousand performers; all manner of instruments were being played, all parts of music were being sung. In one of the grand choruses which sounded through the vast building like a wind from heaven, the keen-eared conductor suddenly threw up his baton and exclaimed, "Flageolet!" In an instant the performance ceased. One of the flageolet players had stopped; something was wanting to the completeness of the performance, and the conductor would not go on. It shall be so in the church. Jesus Christ is conducting His own music. There is indeed a vast volume of resounding harmony rolling upward toward the anthems which fill the heavens; yet if one voice is missing He knows it; if the voice of a little child has ceased He notes the omission; He cannot be satisfied with the mightiest billow which breaks in thunder around His throne, so long as the tiniest wavelet falls elsewhere. Flageolet, where is your tribute? Pealing trumpet, He awaits your blast; sweet cymbals, He desires to hear your silvery chime; mighty organ, unite your many voices in deepening the thunder of the Savior's praise! And if there be one poor sinner who thinks his coarse tones would be out of harmony with such music, let him know that Jesus Christ refines every tribute that is offered in love, and harmonizes the discords of our broken life in the music of His own perfection.

There is one feature in our public Christian life which we should like more fully brought out, and that is the bearing of individual testimony on behalf of Jesus Christ. By no means let us seek to supplant what is known as the regular ministry, but rather supplement it; and at all costs destroy the impression that nobody has a good word to say for Christianity except its paid teachers. Such an impression is, of course, at all times utterly and most cruelly false; yet there is a possibility of so enlarging and strengthening our testimony as to secure the happiest results. Why should not the banker, the great merchant, and the eminent lawyer say publicly what God has done for their souls? If the Prime Minister of England, if the Lord Chancellor, if the judge upon the bench, if the well-known senators would openly testify on behalf of Jesus Christ, they might produce the deepest possible impression for good. Such testimony would destroy the slanderous and blasphemous notion that Christianity is not adapted to the strength, the culture, and the advancement of the present day. It would arrest the attention of genius; it would infuse a new tone into the conversation of the highest circles; it would supply novel material for newspaper comment. We shall be told that this would be "sensationalism"; but let us beware lest the Devil find in

that alarming word one of his easiest victories over
Christian duty and Christian courage. Is it not high time
that there should be sensationalism? Have we not been
troubled with indifference long enough? Has not Jesus
Christ become a merely historical name in many quarters? Terrified by the impotent bugbear of sensationalism; hushed into criminal silence by the possible charge
of sensationalism; frightened into holes and corners lest
anybody should cry "Sensationalism"; living tamely, das-
tardly, shamefacedly, because there is such a word as
sensationalism! Is this manly on our part, or true, or just,
or grateful? If this be sensationalism, how comes it to be
so? Is it not by contrast with long-continued indifference,
with cruel silence, with unholy self-indulgence? Could we
not soon put an end to the charge of sensationalism, by
the strength, the constancy, the ardor of our consecration? Sensationalism is a momentary cry—we may silence it by lifelong continuance in well-doing.

Let those who have social, political, literary, and commercial influence throw it boldly and earnestly into the
cause of Jesus Christ; it is but common justice; having
received much they owe much; and as the time of pay-
ment is brief—alas, how brief! a shadow, a hurrying
wind—let them be prompt if they would be just. Will you
who are full of sin and sorrow throw yourselves at the
Savior's Cross and cry mightily, "God be merciful to me
a sinner"? Wait there until you receive the forgiveness of
your sins. Do not yield to any suggestions to go elsewhere. You will know that you have received the answer
when your hearts are filled with a deep, joyful, unspeakable peace. Will you who have long born the Savior's
name carry the banner of your profession more loftily,
more steadily, and more humbly? Will you who preach
the Gospel give your nights and days to deeper, tenderer
communion with Jesus Christ, desiring of Him the all-
including gift of the Holy Spirit? Will you who are in
business live in the spirit of the golden rule? Will you
who are heads of houses walk before your families in the
fear and love of God? Are you forming the holy vow? In
your heart of hearts are you renewing your covenant

with the Savior? May the word of the Lord prosper; may we know that Christ is gathering many spoils, and realize that the Cross of the Savior is still able to draw men's hearts, and to hold them forever by the omnipotence of love.

Raising Dry Bones

Amzi Clarence Dixon (1854–1925) was a Baptist preacher who ministered to several congregations in the south before becoming pastor of the Moody Memorial Church in Chicago (1906–1911). He left Chicago to pastor the famous Metropolitan Tabernacle in London, "Spurgeon's Tabernacle" (1911–1919). He died in 1925 while pastoring the University Baptist Church, Baltimore, Maryland. A close associate of Reuben A. Torrey, Dixon helped him edit *The Fundamentals*. Dixon was a popular preacher in both Britain and America.

This message is from his book, *Through Night to Morning*, published in 1913.

Amzi Clarence Dixon

8

RAISING DRY BONES

And he said unto me, Son of man, can these bones live?
And I answered, O Lord God, thou knowest (Ezekiel 37:3).

A DRY BONE is a proof of extinct life, for bones are made
only in living organisms. Israel as a nation was once a
living organism full of the life of God. But Israel sinned,
and then came decay with disintegration, until now Israel
has become like a valley of dry bones scattered over the
earth. Man, created in the image of God, was a living
organism filled with the life of God, but man sinned, and
then came decay with disintegration which has made the
world a valley of bones. Now there is no process known to
science by which a dry bone can be suddenly changed into
a living organism. When, therefore, God asked the prophet,
"Can these bones live?" the prophet was compelled to refer
the question back to God for an answer. "O Lord God,
thou and thou alone knowest. If these bones are ever
made to live, thou wilt have to tell us how." And in this
chapter God answers the question as to how dry bones of
all ages may be made to live.

The Prophet's Preparation

In the first place, those commissioned to raise dry bones
must have a special preparation. This preparation is twofold.
One must see a vision of God and receive the touch of God.
In the first chapter of Ezekiel's prophecy we are told that
he saw visions of God! He saw wings with human hands
under them; a vision of the divine and human—the wing
everywhere symbolizes divinity and the hand, humanity—
the divine controlling the human, for the wings moved
the hands. He saw winged creatures with the face of a
man symbolizing intelligence, the face of a lion symbolizing
courage, the face of an ox symbolizing patience, and the

face of an eagle symbolizing aspiration, all under control of the divine wings. The need of every prophet of God is that his intelligence, courage, patience and aspiration shall be linked with God and be completely controlled by Him.

In this vision Ezekiel feels the touch of God. "The hand of the Lord was upon me." The hand of the Lord symbolizes His power, and to be under His hand is to be endued with His power. The Spirit of God is in every Christian for life, but every Christian is not under God's hand for power. The prophet responds to the touch of God and goes where He leads. "The hand of the Lord was upon me and carried me out in the Spirit of the Lord and set me down in the midst of the valley, which was full of bones." He was willing to be led by the Lord's hand into the valley of bones. The temptation is for us to seek the garden with its flowers rather than the valley with its bones.

The prophet also responds when God's hand sets him down in the midst of the bones. Dwelling with the bones is more trying than just going to them on a temporary mission. To have bones for neighbors and companions may not be pleasant. We have a taste for the company of living people. But unless we are ready to respond to the hand of God which would lead us to the bones and make us dwell among them, we are not prepared for the work of raising them to life. The work cannot be done at a distance. The millions who throng the streets, crowd the theaters, drink in saloons and revel in dance halls, shunning the church as they would the pest house, cannot be reached by the pastor in his study making eloquent sermons for his cultured congregation, nor by the Christians who meet in parlors, halls and churches for fellowship and Bible study. Thank God for the men and women who gladly respond to the hand of God leading them to the most sinful and hopeless.

The Test of Faith

Three things severely tested the prophet's faith.

The bones were very many. The valley was white with them. To reach them all by personal effort was impossible. And yet the multitude of the bones did not cause the faith of the prophet to fail, for his eyes were upon God and he believed that God was equal to such a task. As we look at millions unreached by the Gospel, we may be appalled, but the eye of faith sees God still equal to the great work of reaching and saving. No difficulty can surpass His resources.

The bones were very dry. There was no sign of life. Their dryness was positive proof of death. We are apt to classify people as hopeful and hopeless. We are hopeful for the child raised in the Christian family and taught in the Sunday school. We are hopeful for the amiable woman, cultured and refined, who takes an interest in church affairs. But the poor, drunken, shiftless tramp, the hardened criminal, the outcast harlot, and the blatant anarchist, we are apt to regard as hopeless dry bones, if we take our eyes from our God of infinite power and love. If Ezekiel had kept looking at the great number of very dry bones, he might have said, "There is no use trying to raise them to life." But though Ezekiel was willing to face the facts and would not deny the difficulties, he did not look to the bones for assurance of faith. He trusted God who made the men whose bones were before him and who could, by the fiat of His will, remake them. To the man whose faith is in God alone the hopeless becomes hopeful.

The prophet was told to do a very foolish thing. It is foolish to speak to a deaf man, more foolish to speak to a dead man, and it is the climax of folly to speak to a bone so lifeless and formless as not to be classified as man at all. But Ezekiel was willing to appear a fool to the worldly wise. And it is by the foolishness of preaching that men are to be saved.

The Means Used

The man of God spoke the word of God in the power of the Spirit of God. Ezekiel was a man of God in that he was right with God and completely under God's control. It is well to be a man of learning, a man of position, a man of means, a man of eloquence, but it is a thousand times better to be a man of God.

But the word of God must be spoken by the man of

God. The prophet spoke to the bones exactly what God told him. In 2 Timothy 3:16–17, we have the purpose of the Scriptures: "All Scripture is God-breathed, and is profitable for reproof, for correction for instruction in righteousness, that *the man of God* may be complete, thoroughly furnished unto every good work." The man of God has the whole Bible from which to draw equipment for every good work.

But he must be a man of prayer, depending upon the Spirit of God to use the Word. The prophet was commanded to call upon the breath of God to breathe upon the valley of bones, and, while he spoke God's word, God's invisible power moved upon the valley.

Every worker in the valley of bones needs these qualifications. He must be a man of God, a man of the Bible and a man of prayer. He must keep right with God and speak the word of God, while he trusts the Spirit of God. No valley of bones can resist a man of this kind.

The Process

The prophet spoke directly to the bones. There was no manipulation. There was no preparing the bones to receive God's word. He did not try by human wisdom to articulate the bones and cover them with artificial flesh, before he spoke to them and called upon God to move upon them. He knew that bones have no power to receive or retain life. And yet while he spoke, there was a noise; bone came to his bone. The shaking was bone-noise. It was the rattle of death and not the voice of life. Thus dry bones often move and make a deathly noise under the breath of God. When a husband for whom his wife has been praying begins to be especially mean and cruel, I expect him to be converted soon. It is the bones touched by the breath of God and the noise is made by the resistance of his evil heart. When a man for whom I have been praying gets mad and swears at me when I speak to him about His soul, I confidently expect to see him converted in a few days. The bones are moving under the breath of God and the rattling is made by the resistance of his will.

A minister in Boston, that city of cultured bones, told

us in the ministers's meeting, as he discussed the workings of his settlement house, that his workers were not expected to speak of God or Christ. Some of the children had brutal drunkards for fathers, and, if you spoke to them of the fatherhood of God, they would think of God as like their beastly fathers. So you must go down and live with your families among these people and teach them what a true loving father is. Then you can teach them the fatherhood of God and they will understand it. When the speaker was asked if Christ who said, "He that hath seen me hath seen the Father," did not reveal the fatherhood of God better than any earthly father could, and whether, therefore, the preaching of Christ to children with brutal parents would not at once reveal to them what loving fatherhood meant? he seemed puzzled for a reply. What could he say except that he had set aside God's process of revealing His fatherhood and had put in its place a little scheme of his own? His scheme would require years to work and then prove a failure. In the meantime, children are dying without a knowledge of God, while others are growing up as heathen in their relation to God. One day of teaching Christ to these children of the slums will do more to reveal to them the meaning of the fatherhood of God than a decade of looking at the life of any man who lives and shows his faults as well as his virtues in their midst.

What every dry bone of the valley needs, first of all, is a touch of the breath of God. Knowledge of Greek, Latin, French, German, music, mathematics and science leaves spiritual dry bones just as they were. It is the lack of the knowledge of God that makes them dry, and nothing but the knowledge of God can restore them to life.

The Purpose of the Vision

"Ye shall know that I am the Lord." Twice this purpose is given. "Israel herself shall know that I am the Lord, when they shall see that I have raised the valley of scattered bones into an army of living men." There "stood up upon their feet an exceeding great army." Not a great mob like the bones in confusion, but an organized army.

An army carries with it the idea of organization, obedience to orders and leadership under a general. The scattered dry bones of Israel shall become again a living national organism, and the effect of this transformation shall be to make other nations acknowledge the Lord.

The best books now extant on the evidences of Christianity are "the living epistles known and read of all men," who were once moral and spiritual dry bones, but who are now alive and battling in the army of Christ. When in Boston, a young man asked me for a book that would confirm his faith. I told him to go to the men's meeting on Sunday afternoon and listen for half an hour to the testimony of those who had been drunkards and criminals and are now sober, honest, happy husbands and fathers, with the joy of heaven in their faces and the music of heaven in their voices. One live Lazarus is worth forty sermons on the resurrection. Let not the number nor the dryness of the bones appall us. With the vision of God before us and the touch of God upon us, let us speak to them the Word of God while we trust the God of omnipotent power to give them life, and we shall not be disappointed.

NOTES

The Choked Wells

George H. Morrison (1866–1928) assisted the great
Alexander Whyte in Edinburgh, pastored two churches,
and then became pastor in 1902 of the distinguished
Wellington Church on University Avenue in Glasgow,
Scotland. His preaching drew great crowds; in fact, people
had to line up an hour before the services to be sure to get
seats in the large auditorium. Morrison was a master of
imagination in preaching, yet his messages are solidly
biblical.

From his many published volumes of sermons, I have
chosen this message, found in *Flood-Tide*, published in
1904 by Hodder and Stoughton, London.

George H. Morrison

9

THE CHOKED WELLS

And Isaac digged again the wells of water, which they had digged in the days of Abraham his father (Genesis 26:18).

IT IS A STRANGE HISTORY, the history of Isaac. It is full of the lights and shadows, the trials and hopes, that are woven into the web of human life. I rejoice in the full humanity of these old patriarchs. I can never be thankful enough to the Almighty for the exceeding frankness of the Bible. If God had hidden the failings of His children, or sketched them with a halo around their heads as in the dull lives of medieval saints, we should long since have shut this Bible, and let the dust gather on its cover. It lives because the men within it live. It lives because of its wonderful humanity. It is the grace of God in the Lord Jesus Christ inspiring men of like passions with ourselves, that gives the dew of an eternal youth to scripture.

Well, Isaac was a rich and prosperous man when he pitched his tent in the valley of Gerar. And it was in the valley of Gerar, where he dwelt, that he digged again the wells of his father Abraham. Now I want to spiritualize that text tonight. I want to lift it up into the light of Christ. And we shall get to the spiritual worth of it if you will follow me through it in this way. Firstly, the wells of our fathers may get choked: "the Philistines had stopped them after the death of Abraham." Secondly, we must each dig for ourselves to reach the water: "and Isaac digged again the wells of water." Thirdly, our rediscovered wells were named long since: "he called their names after the names by which his father had called them."

The Wells of Our Fathers May Get Choked

You will observe I say they may get choked, not must. There are some wells where men were drinking when the

115

world was young, and where women came with their pitchers on their heads, and sang and drew in the very dawn of history; and spite of all the ages, they are still fresh, and the dripping bucket plashed in them this day. Such was the well of Jacob, for example. And Jesus, weary with His journey, drank of that, though Jacob had been sleeping in his grave for centuries and the traveler still slakes his thirst there. Some wells then, in the preserving providence of God, are never choked.

But the common fate of wells is not like that. Time, changing environment, or even malicious mischief, silts them up. The water is there, but it is hidden, buried. There are well-springs where our fathers slaked their thirst, there were cool waters for their parched souls, there were deep places shadowed from the glare, and they drew comfort and power and hope out of the depths. And the children need to be refreshed just as their fathers did; but somehow the old wells have got choked for them.

Perhaps the most signal instance of that choking the world has ever seen was the law of Moses in the time of Christ. Once, in the golden days of Israel, the law of Moses had been a well of water. Men had looked down into its strange deeps, and seen reflected in the waters of it something of heaven. It was not wine—it was not the wine of the Gospel. But, at least, it was water for the thirsty soul. Then came the Pharisees—and a Pharisee is the worst Philistine under heaven—then came the Pharisees and Jewish lawyers, and buried God's simple law in such a mass of learned human folly, poured such a cargo of sand upon that spring, that the wells were choked, and the waters that their fathers drank were lost. And souls would have perished of thirst, but for Jesus Christ.

And have we not found the same thing in the Gospel? There is nothing more tragic in the history of Christianity than the silting and choking of our fathers' wells.

Take the great central doctrine of the sacrifice on Calvary. What a joy, what a power there was in that for the men who perused the letters of the New Testament. What a sweet and unexplained simplicity about it to the first hearts to whom the tidings came. It was the gladdest news that ever cheered the world, that Jesus died on Calvary for men. But by and by that well got silted up. It became filled with intolerable views of God; it was buried under degrading views of man. The well was choked. The Philistines had done it. And the children went thirsty where their fathers drank.

Think of the sacraments. Do you want to know the blessings of a sacrament? Go and ask the Ethiopian eunuch that, as he mounts his chariot again after his baptism. Do you wish to see the comfort of a sacrament? Go and read the story of the primitive church again, when the disciples broke bread from house to house. The sacraments were wells in that bright morning, where the humblest follower of Jesus Christ could drink. They were cool places, with the green fern rooting in the shadow, and the waters of rest within, far down, beneath. And when I think how that simple ritual has been degraded, how the bitterest quarrels of an angry Christendom have centered and screamed around the bread and wine, I see how the wells of our fathers may get choked.

Think of the Bible. I thank God that for many a heart that well is still unchoked. I am glad that there are men and women here tonight who are not ignorant, who are not afraid of the truth nor of the light, and the Word of God is still their guide. But here is a young fellow, and he is one of thousands, or a young woman, and she is one of hundreds—and you were trained in a home where the Bible was daily read, and you caught the flavor of it in your father's speech; and you cannot think of your mother but you see the Bible open on her knee, and what a heroine your mother was you know. And you, O son, O daughter, of old-fashioned parents, whose shoe-latchets you are unworthy to unloose—for *you* that well of the ages has been choked. It may be doubt has done it. It may be the storm of criticism that is raging. It may be that mass impertinent literature that is keeping us back from what is pure and good. Whatever the cause, the well of your fathers has been choked for you. You never get help or strength or courage there.

We Must Each Dig for Ourselves
to Reach the Water

Of all the parables that Jesus spoke, if we except that
of the prodigal son, I think the most wonderful, for its
intensity and power, is the story of the house built on the
rock. Now, there is one fine touch in that fine parable
that is almost lost in our English version. It is where we
are told the man digged deep. But the expression is far
stronger than digged deep. It is, he digged, and kept on
deepening. And the picture is of a man who takes his
spade, and he says, There is rock down here, and I shall
reach it. And he digs and deepens, and he deepens and
digs, and the sweat falls, and he is weary, but he digs;
and he strikes on the solid rock at last, and builds there,
and when the tempest burst—you know. And was there
no rock under the sand as well? Was there no solid basis
where the *other* built? Yes, hidden under the sand, deep
down, was rock. But he refused to dig for it himself: he
was too sluggish and inert to go on deepening; he took
things as he found them, built on what lay to hand; and
when the storm broke—you know.

And one great blight upon the church today is just that
men and women will not dig. They are either content to
accept their father's creed, or they are content, on the
strength of arguments a child could answer, to cast it
overboard. But to bend down and dig, to vow before heaven
only to build on rock, and then to believe that, in a universe like this, with God in heaven, somewhere there
must be rock to build my life on, and somewhere there
must be water for my soul to drink—that high enthusiasm and new endeavor breathed upon you, brother, by
the spirit of Jesus, would establish you, make a man of
you, and send a thrill into the church of God.

And you can always tell when a man has been digging
for himself by the freshness, the individuality of his religion. All we like sheep have gone astray, and it is very
hard to tell one sheep from another. But in our father's
home we are all children, and what a world of difference
between each one! Could you ever confuse the apostle
John with Peter? Did you ever read James and think you

were studying Paul? It is the hypocrites who are tarred with the same stick. It is the surface-Christians who cannot afford to be original. The humblest souls, if they have dug for themselves, and by their own search have found the water, will have a note in their music that was never heard before, and some discovery of God that is their own.

That leads me to our third thought for tonight. Our first was to remember that the wells of our fathers may get choked. And our second was that we each must dig for ourselves to find the water. Here is our third and last.

Our Rediscovered Wells Were Named Long Since

When Isaac dug his wells at Gerar, men had forgotten about the wells of Abraham. And as Isaac dug and rounded out the basins, there was not a man of them but thought this was a new work. But the day came when Isaac named his wells. And when the neighbors gathered and asked him what the names were, they found they were names that had been given by Abraham. And then the past would flash on them again. They would remember how on these very spots, when they were children, Abraham had dug and drank. The wells were not new. They were but rediscovered. And the rediscovered wells were named long since.

Now if I am in earnest about the higher life, I seem to be always finding some new well. I come on them strangely, unexpectedly. I dig and discover the cool water there. There is an element of sweet surprise, there is a constant wonder and a constant freshness in it, when I am fighting my own way to God and heaven. Who thinks that the life of religion is monotonous? There is no novel so full of novelties as it. New truths flash out on me. New prospects summon me. I am thrilled with the unexpected things that dawn on me when I am pressing with heart and soul toward the mark. I never pray but a new light is given. I never dig but a new well is found. And we think at first these wells are all our own. We think at first that never one single soul out of the twice ten thousand who have gone before us had ever any experience of this. It is our well, it is our discovery, it is a new thing! It is quite unnamed. But the day comes when we find it is not so.

The rediscovered wells were named long since. They are the very waters that our fathers drank; but the toil and effort, the struggle and the prayer that it took us to reach them, made them so fresh to us that we thought they were a new thing in the world.

And therefore I say to every young man and woman here tonight: Be utterly fearless in the pursuit of truth. And if it be the craving for the best that fires you, and the true longing to be at peace with God, you will make great discoveries, my brother, and they will all be wonderful to you, and you will live to find they were all known and named when Abraham pitched his tent beside Beersheba. You remember the old legend of *Quo Vadis?* You remember how Peter, flying from persecution at Rome, was met by a figure—it was Jesus' figure—and asked *Quo vadis?*— Whither goest thou, Peter? So many a father is asking of his son, and many a mother is asking of her daughter, *Quo vadis?*—whither goest thou? And out into the desert may be the answer, searching for peace, searching for God! But the search will lead to the old waters yet, and the digging will draw to the ancient wells again.

NOTES

How to Promote a Revival

Charles Grandison Finney (1792–1875) was one of America's leading revivalists. During his ministry people were converted by the thousands and their lives were radically changed. He was a successful lawyer in Adams, New York, when he was converted in 1821. He served as a Presbyterian home missionary from 1824 to 1832 when he became pastor of Second Free Church in New York City. Unhappy with Presbyterian government and theology, he accepted a call to the Congregational Broadway Tabernacle in New York City in 1834, and the next year became Professor of Theology at Oberlin College, Oberlin, Ohio. In 1852, he became president of the school. His preaching was used of God during the Great Revival of 1858–59, during which an estimated 600,000 people turned to Christ. He was a courageous preacher who believed that God would send spiritual awakening if God's people would only meet the conditions.

This sermon is from *Lectures on Revival of Religion*, published by Fleming H. Revell in 1888.

Charles Grandison Finney

10

HOW TO PROMOTE A REVIVAL

Break up your fallow ground; for it is time to seek the Lord, till he come and rain righteousness upon you (Hosea 10:12).

THE JEWS WERE a nation of farmers, and it is therefore a common thing in the Scriptures to refer for illustrations to their occupation, and to the scenes with which farmers and shepherds are familiar. The prophet Hosea addresses them as a nation of backsliders, and reproves them for their idolatry, and threatens them with the judgments of God. I have showed you in my first lecture what a revival is not, what it is, and the agencies to be employed in promoting it; in my second, when it is needed, its importance, and when it may be expected. My design in this lecture is to show,

How a Revival Is to Be Promoted

A revival consists of two parts; as it respects the church, and as it respects the ungodly. I shall speak tonight of a revival in the church. Fallow ground is ground which has once been tilled but which now lies waste, and needs to be broken up and mellowed before it is suited to receive grain. I shall show, as it respects a revival in the church,

1. What it is to break up the fallow ground, in the sense of the text.
2. How it is to be performed.

What Is It to Break Up the Fallow Ground?

To break up the fallow ground is to *break up your hearts*—to prepare your minds to bring forth fruit to God. The mind of man is often compared in the Bible to ground, and the Word of God to seed sown in it, and the fruit represents the actions and affections of those who receive

it. To break up the fallow ground, therefore, is to bring
the mind into such a state that it is fitted to receive the
Word of God. Sometimes your hearts get matted down
hard and dry, and all run to waste, until there is no such
thing as getting fruit from them until they are all broken
up, and mellowed down, and fitted to receive the Word of
God. It is this softening of the heart, so as to make it feel
the truth, which the prophet calls breaking up your fallow ground.

How Is the Fallow Ground to Be Broken Up?

It is not by any direct efforts to feel. People run into a
mistake on this subject, from not making the laws of
mind the object of thought. There are great errors on the
subject of the laws which govern the mind. People talk
about religious feeling as if they thought they could, by
direct effort, call forth religious affection. But this is not
the way the mind acts. No man can make himself feel in
this way merely by *trying* to feel. The feelings of the mind
are not *directly* under our control. We cannot by willing,
or by direct volition, call forth religious feelings. We might
as well think to call spirits up from the deep. They are
purely involuntary states of mind. They naturally and
necessarily exist in the mind under certain circumstances
calculated to excite them. But they can be controlled *indi-
rectly.* Otherwise there would be no moral character in
our feelings if there were not a way to control them. We
cannot say, "Now I will feel so and so toward such an
object." But we can command our *attention* to it, and look
at it intently, until the involuntary affections arise. Let a
man who is away from his family bring them up before
his mind, and will he not feel? But it is not by saying to
himself, "Now I will feel deeply for my family." A man can
direct his attention to any object about which he ought to
feel and wishes to feel, and in that way he will call into
existence the proper emotions. Let a man call up his enemy before his mind, and his feelings of enmity will rise.
So if a man thinks of God, and fastens his mind on any
part of God's character, he will feel—emotions will come
up, by the very laws of mind. If he is a friend of God, let

him contemplate God as a gracious and holy being, and he will have emotions of friendship kindled up in his mind. If he is an enemy of God, only let him get the true character of God before his mind, and look at it, and fasten his attention on it, and his enmity will rise against God, or he will break down and give his heart to God.

If you wish to break up the fallow ground of your hearts, and make your minds feel on the subject of religion, you must go to work just as you would to feel on any other subject. Instead of keeping your thoughts on everything else, and then imagine that by going to a few meetings you will get your feelings enlisted, go the common sense way to work, as you would on any other subject. It is just as easy to make your minds feel on the subject of religion as it is on any other subject. God has put these states of mind under your control. If people were as unphilosophical about moving their limbs as they are about regulating their emotions, you would never have gotten here to meeting tonight.

If you mean to break the fallow ground of your hearts, you must begin by looking at your hearts—examine and note the state of your minds, and see where you are. Many never seem to think about this. They pay no attention to their own hearts, and never know whether they are doing well in religion or not, whether they are gaining ground or going back, whether they are fruitful, or lying waste like the fallow ground. Now you must draw off your attention from other things, and look into this. Make a business of it. Do not be in a hurry. Examine thoroughly the state of your hearts, and see where you are; whether you are walking with God every day, or walking with the Devil; whether you are serving God or serving the Devil most; whether you are under the dominion of the prince of darkness, or of the Lord Jesus Christ.

To do all this, you must set yourselves at work to consider your sins. You must examine yourselves. And by this I do not mean that you must stop and look directly within to see what is the present state of your feelings. That is the very way to put a stop to all feeling. This is just as absurd as it would be for a man to shut his eyes on the lamp and try to turn his eyes inward to find out whether there was any image painted on the retina. The man complains that he does not see anything! And why? Because he has turned his eyes away from the objects of sight. The truth is, our moral feelings are as much an object of consciousness as our sensations. And the way to excite them is to go on acting and employing our minds. Then we can tell our moral feelings by consciousness, just as I could tell my natural feelings by consciousness, if I should put my hand in the fire.

Self-examination consists in looking at your lives, in considering your actions, in calling up the past, and learning its true character. Look back over your past history. Take up your individual sins one by one, and look at them. I do not mean that you should just cast a glance at your past life, and see that it has been full of sins, and then go to God and make a sort of general confession, and ask for pardon. That is not the way. You must take them up one by one. It will be a good thing to take a pen and paper, as you go over them, and write them down as they occur to you. Go over them as carefully as a merchant goes over his books; as often as a sin comes before your memory, add it to the list. General confessions of sin will never do. Your sins were committed *one by one*; as far as you can come at them, they ought to be reviewed and repented of one by one. Now begin; and take up first what are commonly, but *improperly*, called your

Sins of Omission

1. *Ingratitude.* Take this sin, for instance, and write down under it all the instances you can remember wherein you have received favors from God for which you have never exercised gratitude. How many cases can you remember? Some remarkable providence, some wonderful turn of events, that saved you from ruin. Set down the instances of God's goodness to you when you were in sin, before your conversion. Then the mercy of God in the circumstances of your conversion, for which you have never been half thankful enough. The numerous mercies you have received since. How long the catalog of instances

where your ingratitude is so black that you are forced to hide your face in confusion! Now go on your knees, and confess them one by one to God, and ask forgiveness. The very act of confession, by the laws of suggestion, will bring up others to your memory. Put down these. Go over these three or four times in this way, and you will find an astonishing amount of mercies for which you have never thanked God. Then take another sin.

2. *Want of love to God.* Write that down, and go over all the instances you can remember when you did not give to the blessed God that hearty love which you ought. Think how grieved and alarmed you would be if you discovered any flagging of affection for you in your wife, husband, or children; if you saw somebody else engrossing their hearts, and thoughts, and time. Perhaps, in such a case, you would well nigh die with a just and virtuous jealousy. Now, God styles Himself a jealous God; and have you not given your heart to other loves, played the harlot, and infinitely offended Him?

3. *Neglect of the Bible.* Put down the cases when for days, and perhaps for weeks—yes, it may be even for months together—you had no pleasure in God's Word. Perhaps you did not read a chapter, or if you read it, it was in a way that was still more displeasing to God. Many people read over a whole chapter in such a way that if they were put under oath when they have done, they could not tell what they have been reading. With so little attention do they read that they cannot remember where they have read from morning until evening, unless they put in a string or turn down a leaf. This demonstrates that they did not lay to heart what they read, that they did not make it a subject of reflection. If you were reading a novel, or any other piece of intelligence that greatly interested you, would you not remember what you read last? And the fact that you fold a leaf or put in a string demonstrates that you read rather as a task than from love or reverence for the Word of God. The Word of God is the rule of your duty. And do you pay so little regard to it as not to remember what you read? If so, no wonder that you live so at random, and that your religion is such a miserable failure.

4. *Unbelief.* Instances in which you have virtually charged the God of truth with lying by your unbelief of His express promises and declarations. God has promised to give the Holy Spirit to them that ask Him. Now, have you believed this? Have you expected Him to answer? Have you not virtually said in your hearts when you prayed for the Holy Spirit, "I do not believe that I shall receive it"? If you have not believed nor expected you should receive the blessing, which God has expressly promised, you have charged Him with lying.

5. *Neglect of prayer.* Times when you omitted secret prayer, family prayer, and prayer meetings, or have prayed in such a way as more grievously to offend God than to have neglected it altogether.

6. *Neglect of the means of grace.* When you have suffered trifling excuses to prevent your attending meetings, have neglected and poured contempt upon the means of salvation, merely from disrelish of spiritual duties.

7. *The manner in which you have performed* those duties—want of feeling—want of faith—worldly frame of mind—so that your words were nothing but the mere chattering of a wretch that did not deserve that God should feel the least care for Him. When you have fallen down upon your knees, and *said your prayers* in such an unfeeling and careless manner that if you had been put under oath five minutes after you left your closet, you could not have told what you had been praying for.

8. *Want of love for the souls of your fellowmen.* Look around upon your friends and relations, and remember how little compassion you have felt for them. You have stood by and seen them going right to hell, and it seems as though you did not care if they did. How many days have there been in which you did not make their condition the subject of a single fervent prayer, or even an ardent desire for their salvation?

9. *Want of care for the heathen.* Perhaps you have not cared enough for them to attempt to learn their condition; perhaps not even to take a missionary paper. Look at this, and see how much you do really care for the heathen, and set down honestly the real amount of your

feelings for them, and your desire for their salvation. Measure your desire for their salvation by the self-denial you practice in giving of your substance to send them the Gospel. Do you deny yourself even the hurtful superfluities of life, such as tea, coffee, and tobacco? Do you retrench your style of living and really subject yourself to any inconvenience to save them? Do you daily pray for them in your closet? Do you statedly attend the monthly concert? Are you from month to month laying by something to put into the treasury of the Lord when you go up to pray? If you are not doing these things, and if your soul is not agonized for the poor benighted heathen, why are you such a hypocrite as to pretend to be a Christian? Why, your profession is an insult to Jesus Christ!

10. *Neglect of family duties.* How you have lived before them, how you have prayed, what an example you have set before them. What direct efforts do you habitually make for their spiritual good? What duty have you not neglected?

11. *Neglect of social duties.*

12. *Neglect of watchfulness over your own life.* Instances in which you have hurried over your private duties and not taken yourself to task, nor honestly made up your accounts with God. Where you have entirely neglected to watch your conduct, and have been off your guard, and have sinned before the world, and before the church, and before God.

13. *Neglect to watch over your brethren.* How often have you broken your covenant that you would watch over them in the Lord! How little do you know or care about the state of their souls! And yet you are under a solemn oath to watch over them. What have you done to make yourself acquainted with them? How many of them have you interested yourself in to know their spiritual state? Go over the list, and wherever you find there has been a neglect, write it down. How many times have you seen your brethren growing cold in religion, and have not spoken to them about it? You have seen them beginning to neglect one duty after another, and you did not

reprove them in a brotherly way. You have seen them falling into sin, and you let them go on. And yet you pretend to love them. What a hypocrite! Would you see your wife or child going into disgrace, or into the fire, and hold your peace? No, you would not. What do you think of yourself, then, to pretend to love Christians, and to love Christ, while you can see them going into disgrace, and say nothing to them?

14. *Neglect of self-denial.* There are many professors who are willing to do almost anything in religion that does not require self-denial. But when they are called to do anything that requires them to deny themselves, Oh! that is too much. They think they are doing a great deal for God, and doing about as much as He ought to ask in reason, if they are only doing what they can do about as well as not, but they are not willing to deny themselves any comfort or convenience whatever for the sake of serving the Lord. They will not willingly suffer reproach for the name of Christ. Nor will they deny themselves the *luxuries* of life to save a world from hell. So far are they from remembering that self-denial is a *condition of discipleship* that they do not know what self-denial is. They never have really denied themselves a ribbon or a pin for Christ, and for the Gospel. Oh, how soon such professors will be in hell! Some are giving of *their abundance*, and are giving much, and are ready to complain that others don't give more; when, in truth, they do not give anything that they *need*, anything that they could enjoy, if they kept it. They only give of their surplus wealth; and perhaps that poor woman who puts in twelve and a half cents at the monthly concert has exercised more self-denial, than they have in giving thousands.

Sins of Commission

1. *Worldly mindedness.* What has been the state of your heart in regard to your worldly possessions? Have you looked at them as really *yours*—as if you had a right to dispose of them as your own, according to your own will? If you have, write that down. If you have loved property, and sought after it for its own sake, or to gratify lust

or ambition, or a worldly spirit, or to lay it up for your families, you have sinned, and must repent.

2. *Pride.* Recollect all the instances you can in which you have detected yourself in the exercise of pride. Vanity is a particular form of pride. How many times have you detected yourself in consulting vanity about your dress and appearance? How many times have you thought more, and taken more pains, and spent more time, about decorating your body to go to church than you have about preparing your mind for the worship of God? You have gone to the house of God caring more how you appear outwardly in the sight of mortal men than how your soul appears in the sight of the heart-searching God. You have in fact set up yourself to be worshiped by them, rather than prepared to worship God yourself. You came to divide the worship of God's house, to draw off the attention of God's people to look at your pretty appearance. It is in vain to pretend now that you don't care anything about having people look at you. Be honest about it. Would you take all these pains about your looks if everybody was blind?

3. *Envy.* Look at the cases in which you were envious at those who you thought were above you in any respect. Or perhaps you have envied those who have been more talented or more useful than yourself. Have you not so envied some, that you have been pained to hear them praised? It has been more agreeable to you to dwell upon their faults, than upon their virtues, upon their failures, than upon their success. Be honest with yourself, and if you have harbored this spirit of hell, repent deeply before God, or *He will never forgive you.*

4. *Censoriousness.* Instances in which you have had a bitter spirit, and spoken of Christians in a manner entirely devoid of charity and love—charity, which requires you always to hope the best the case will admit, and to put the best construction upon any ambiguous conduct.

5. *Slander.* The times you have spoken behind people's backs of their faults, real or supposed, of members of the church or others, unnecessarily or without good reason. This is slander. You need not lie to be guilty of slander— to tell the truth with the design to injure, is slander.

6. *Levity.* How often have you trifled before God, as you would not have dared to trifle in the presence of an earthly sovereign? You have either been an atheist, and forgotten that there was a God, or have had less respect for Him, and His presence, than you would have had for an earthly judge.

7. *Lying.* Understand now what lying is. Any species of *designed* deception for a selfish reason is lying. If the deception is not a design, it is not lying. But if you design to make an impression contrary to the naked truth, you lie. Put down all those cases you can recollect. Don't call them by any soft name. God calls them *lies*, and charges you with *lying*, and you had better charge yourself correctly.

How innumerable are the falsehoods perpetrated everyday in business and in social intercourse, by words, looks, and actions—designed to make an impression on others contrary to the truth for selfish reasons.

8. *Cheating.* Set down all the cases in which you have dealt with an individual and done to him that which you would not like to have done to you. *That* is cheating. God has laid down a rule in the case: "All things whatsoever ye would that men should do to you, do ye even so to them." That is the rule; now if you have not done so you are a cheat. Mind, the rule is not that you should do what you might reasonably expect them to do to you. That is a rule which would admit of every degree of wickedness. But it is "As ye *would* they should do to you."

9. *Hypocrisy.* For instance, in your prayers and confessions to God. Set down the instances in which you have prayed for things you did not really want. And the evidence is that when you have done praying, you could not tell what you had prayed for. How many times have you confessed sins that you did not mean to break off and when you had no solemn purpose not to repeat them? Yes, have confessed sins when you knew you as much expected to go and repeat them as you expected to live.

10. *Robbing God.* Instances in which you have misspent your time and squandered hours which God gave you to serve Him and save souls in vain amusements or foolish conversation, reading novels, or doing nothing; cases where you have misapplied your talents and powers of

mind; where you have squandered money on your lusts, or spent it for things you did not need, and which neither contributed to your health, comfort, or usefulness. Perhaps some of you who are here tonight have laid out God's money for *tobacco*. I will not speak of rum, for I presume there is no professor of religion here tonight that would drink rum. I hope there is no one that uses the filthy poison, tobacco. Think of a professor of religion using God's money to poison himself with tobacco!

11. *Bad temper.* Perhaps you have abused your wife, or your children, or your family, or servants, or neighbors. Write it all down.

12. *Hindering others from being useful.* Perhaps you have weakened their influence by insinuations against them. You have not only robbed God of your own talents, but tied the hands of somebody else. What a wicked servant is he that loiters himself and hinders the rest! This is done sometimes by taking their time needlessly; sometimes by destroying Christian confidence in them. Thus you have played into the hands of Satan, and not only showed yourself an idle vagabond, but prevented others from working.

If you find you have committed a fault against an individual, and that individual is within your reach, go and confess it immediately, and get that out of the way. If the individual you have injured is too far off for you to go and see him, sit down and write him a letter, and confess the injury, *pay the postage*, and put it into the mail immediately. I say, pay the postage, or otherwise you will only make the matter worse. You will add to the former injury by making him a bill of expense. The man that writes a letter on his own business, and sends it to another without paying the postage is dishonest and has cheated him out of so much. And if he would cheat a man out of a sixpence or shilling, when the temptation is so small, what would he not do were the temptation greater if he had the prospect of impunity? If you have defrauded anybody, send the money, the full amount and the interest.

Go thoroughly to work in all this. Go *now*. Don't put it off; that will only make the matter worse. Confess to God those sins that have been committed against God, and to man those sins that have been committed against man. Don't think of getting off by going around the stumbling blocks. Take them up out of the way. In breaking up your fallow ground, you must remove every obstruction. Things may be left that you may think little things, and you may wonder why you do not feel as you wish to in religion, when the reason is that your proud and carnal mind has covered up something which God required you to confess and remove. Break up all the ground and turn it over. Do not balk it, as the farmers say; do not turn aside for little difficulties; drive the plow right through them, beam deep, and turn the ground all up, so that it may all be mellow and soft, and fit to receive the seed and bear fruit a hundredfold.

When you have gone over your whole history in this way, thoroughly, if you will then go over the ground the second time, and give your solemn and fixed attention to it, you will find that the things you have put down will suggest other things of which you have been guilty, connected with them, or near them. Then go over it a third time, and you will recollect other things connected with these. And you will find in the end that you can remember an amount of your history, and particular actions, even in this life, which you did not think you should remember in eternity. Unless you do take up your sins in this way, and consider them in detail, one by one, you can form no idea of the amount of your sins. You should go over it as thoroughly, carefully, and solemnly as you would if you were just preparing yourself for the judgment.

As you go over the catalog of your sins be sure to resolve upon present and entire reformation. Wherever you find anything wrong, resolve at once, in the strength of God, to sin no more in that way. It will be of no benefit to examine yourself unless you determine to amend in *every particular* that you find wrong in heart, temper, or conduct.

If you find, as you go on with this duty, that your mind is still all dark, cast about you, and you will find there is some reason for the Spirit of God to depart from you. You have not been faithful and thorough. In the progress of such a work you have got to do violence to yourself, and bring yourself as a rational being up to this work with the Bible before you and try your heart until you *do* feel. You need not expect that God will work a miracle for you to break up your fallow ground. It is to be done by means. Fasten your attention to the subject of your sins. You cannot look at your sins long and thoroughly, and see how bad they are without feeling, and feeling deeply. Experience abundantly proves the benefit of going over our history in this way. Set yourself to the work now; resolve that you never will stop until you find you can *pray*. You never will have the spirit of prayer until you examine yourself, and confess your sins, and break up your fallow ground. You never will have the Spirit of God dwelling in you until you have unraveled this whole mystery of iniquity and spread out your sins before God. Let there be this deep work of repentance and full confession, this breaking down before God, and you will have as much of the spirit of prayer as your body can bear up under. The reason why so few Christians know anything about the spirit of prayer is because they never would take the pains to examine themselves properly, and so never knew what it was to have their hearts all broken up in this way.

You see I have only begun to lay open this subject tonight. I want to lay it out before you in the course of these lectures, so that if you will begin and go on to do as I say, the results will be just as certain as they are when the farmer breaks up a fallow field, and mellows it, and sows his grain. It will be so, if you will only begin in this way, and hold on until all your hardened and callous hearts break up.

Remarks

1. It will do no good to preach to you while your hearts are in this hardened and waste and fallow state. The farmer might just as well sow his grain on the rock. It will bring forth no fruit. This is the reason why there are so many fruitless professors in the church, and why there is so much outside machinery, and so little deep-toned feeling in the

church. Look at the Sunday school for instance, and see how much machinery there is, and how little of the power of godliness. If you go on in this way, the Word of God will continue to harden you, and you will grow worse and worse, just as the rain and snow on an old fallow field makes the turf thicker and the clods stronger.

2. See why so much preaching is wasted, and worse than wasted. It is because the church will not break up their fallow ground. A preacher may wear out his life, and do very little good while there are so many stony-ground hearers who have never had their fallow ground broken up. They are only half converted, and their religion is rather a change of opinion than a change of the feeling of their hearts. There is mechanical religion enough, but very little that looks like deep heart work.

3. Professors of religion should never satisfy themselves, or expect a revival, just by starting out of their slumbers and blustering about and making a noise and talking to sinners. They must get their fallow ground broken up. It is utterly unphilosophical to think of getting engaged in religion in this way. If your fallow ground is broken up, then the way to get more feeling is to go out and see sinners on the road to hell, and talk to them, and guide inquiring souls, and you will get more feeling. You may get into an *excitement* without this breaking up; you may show a kind of zeal, but it will not last long, and it will not take hold of sinners, unless your hearts are broken up. The reason is that you go about it mechanically and have not broken up your fallow ground.

4. And now, finally, will you break up your fallow ground? Will you enter upon the course now pointed out, and persevere until you are thoroughly awake? If you fail here, if you do not do *this* and get prepared, you can go no further with me in this course of lectures. I have gone with you as far as it is of any use to go until your fallow ground is broken up. Now, you must make thorough work upon this point, or all I have further to say will do you little good. No, it will only harden and make you worse. If, when next Friday night arrives, it finds you with unbroken hearts, you need not expect to be benefited by what I shall

say. If you do not set about this work immediately, I shall take it for granted that you do not mean to be revived, that you have forsaken your minister and mean to let him go up to battle alone. If you do not do this, I charge you with having forsaken Christ, with refusing to repent and do your first work. But if you will be prepared to enter upon the work, I propose, God willing, next Friday evening, to lead you into the work of saving sinners.

How Christ Came to Church

Adoniram Judson Gordon (1836–1895) pastored the Clarendon Street Baptist Church in Boston from 1869 to 1895 and boldly preached the orthodox faith while many pulpiteers were yielding to the "new truths" of evolution and "higher criticism." He was a vigorous promoter of missions and prophetic teaching, and his ministry led to the founding of Gordon College and Gordon-Conwell Seminary. "How Christ Came to Church" was born out of a dream Dr. Gordon had that made a deep impression on him. He was careful to point out that the dream was not a "new revelation" but only contained a special lesson he needed to learn from God.

This version is from *The Great Pulpit Masters: A. J. Gordon*, published in 1951 by Fleming H. Revell.

Adoniram Judson Gordon

11

HOW CHRIST CAME TO CHURCH

IT WAS SATURDAY NIGHT, when wearied from the work of preparing Sunday's sermon, that I fell asleep and the dream came. I was in the pulpit before a full congregation, just ready to begin my sermon, when a stranger entered and passed slowly up the left aisle of the church, looking first to the one side and then to the other as though silently asking with his eyes that someone would give him a seat. He had proceeded nearly halfway up the aisle when a gentleman stepped out and offered him a place in his pew, which was quietly accepted. Except the face and features of the stranger, everything in the scene is distinctly remembered—the number of the pew, the Christian man who offered his hospitality, the exact seat which was occupied. Only the countenance of the visitor could never be recalled. That his face wore a peculiarly serious look, as of one who had known some great sorrow, is clearly impressed on my mind. His bearing, too, was exceeding humble, his dress poor and plain, and from the beginning to the end of the service he gave the most respectful attention to the preacher. Immediately as I began my sermon my attention became riveted on this hearer. If I would avert my eyes from him for a moment they would instinctively return to him, so that he held my attention rather than I held his until the discourse was ended.

To myself I said constantly, "Who can that stranger be?" and then I mentally resolved to find out by going to him and making his acquaintance as soon as the service should be over. But after the benediction had been given, the departing congregation filed into the aisles and before I could reach him the visitor had left the house. The gentleman with whom he had sat remained behind, however, and approaching him with great eagerness I asked,

"Can you tell me who that stranger was who sat in your pew this morning?" In the most matter-of-course way he replied: "Why, do you not know that man? It was Jesus of Nazareth." With a sense of the keenest disappointment, I said: "My dear sir, why did you let Him go without introducing me to Him? I was so desirous to speak with Him." And with the same nonchalant air the gentleman replied: "Oh, do not be troubled. He has been here today, and no doubt He will come again."

And now came an indescribable rush of emotion. As when a strong current is suddenly checked, the stream rolls back upon itself and is choked in its own foam, so the intense curiosity which had been going out toward the mysterious hearer now returned upon the preacher: and the Lord Himself "whose I am and whom I serve" had been listening to me today. What was I saying? Was I preaching on some popular theme in order to catch the ear of the public? Well, thank God, it was of Himself I was speaking. However imperfectly done, it was Christ and Him crucified whom I was holding up this morning. But in what spirit did I preach? Was it "Christ crucified preached in a crucified style?" Or did the preacher magnify himself while exalting Christ? So anxious and painful did these questionings become that I was about to ask the brother with whom He had sat if the Lord had said anything to him concerning the sermon, but a sense of propriety and self-respect at once checked the suggestion. Then immediately other questions began with equal vehemence to crowd into the mind. "What did He think of our sanctuary, its Gothic arches, its stained windows, its costly and powerful organ? How was He impressed with the music and the order of the worship?" It did not seem at that moment as though I could ever again care or have the smallest curiosity as to what men might say of preaching, worship, or church, if I only could know that He had not been displeased, that He would not withhold His feet from coming again because He had been grieved at what He might have seen or heard.

We speak of "a momentous occasion." This, though in sleep, was recognized as such by the dreamer—a lifetime, almost an eternity, of interest crowded into a single solemn moment. One present for an hour who could tell me all I have so longed to know, who could point out to me the imperfections of my service, who could reveal to me my real self, to whom, perhaps, I am most a stranger; who could correct the errors in our worship to which long usage and accepted tradition may have rendered us insensible. While I had been preaching for a half hour, He had been here and listening who could have told me all this and infinitely more—and my eyes had been holden that I knew Him not; and now He had gone. "Yet a little while I am with you and then I go unto him that sent me."

One thought, however, lingered in my mind with something of comfort and more of awe. *"He has been here today, and no doubt He will come again"*; and mentally repeating these words as one regretfully meditating on a vanished vision, "I awoke, and it was a dream." No, it was not a dream. It was a vision of the deepest reality, a miniature of an actual ministry, verifying the statement often repeated that sometimes we are most awake toward God when we are asleep toward the world.

"Here today, and to come again." In this single sentence the two critical turning points of an extended ministry are marked. It is not what we have but what we know that we have which determines our material or spiritual wealth. A poor farmer owned a piece of hard, rocky land from which, at the price of only the severest toil, he was able to support his family. He died and bequeathed his farm to his eldest son. By an accident the son discovered traces of gold on the land which, being explored, was found to contain mineral wealth of immense value. The father had had precisely the same property which the son now possessed, but while the one lived and died a poor man, the other became independently rich. And yet the difference between the two depended entirely upon the fact that the son knew what he had, and the father did not know. "Where two or three are gathered in my name *there am I in the midst of them*," says Christ.

Then the dream was literally true, was it? Yes. If this promise of the Son of God means what it says, Jesus of Nazareth was present not only on that Sunday morning, but on every Sunday morning when His disciples assemble for worship. "Why, then, oh, preacher, did you not fix your attention on Him from the first day you stood up in the congregation as His witness, asking how you might please Him before once raising the question how you might please the people, and how in your ministry you might have His help above the help of every other? Was the dream which came to you in the transient visions of the night more real to you than His own promise, 'Lo, I am with you always,' which is given in that word which endures forever?" Alas, that it was ever so! It is not what we know but what we know that we know which constitutes our spiritual wealth. I must have read and expounded these words of Jesus again and again during my ministry, but, somehow, for years they had no really practical meaning to me. Then came a blessed and ever-to-be-remembered crisis in my spiritual life, when from a deeper insight into Scripture the doctrine of the Holy Spirit began to open to me. Now I apprehended how and in what sense Jesus is present: not in some figurative or even potential sense, but literally and really present in the Holy Spirit, His invisible self. "And I will pray the Father, and he shall give you another Comforter, that he *may abide with you forever*" (John 14:16). The coming of this other Paraclete was conditioned on the departure of Jesus: "If I go I will send him unto you." And this promise was perfectly fulfilled on Pentecost. As truly as Christ went up, the Holy Ghost came down: the one took His place at the Father's right hand in heaven, the other took His seat in the church on earth which is "builded together for a habitation of God in the Spirit." And yet, lest by this discourse about His going and the Comforter's coming we should be led to think that it is not Christ who is with us, He says, clearly referring to the Spirit: "I will not leave you orphans; *I will come to you.*" Thus it is made plain that the Lord Himself is truly though invisibly here in the midst of every company of disciples gathered in any place in His name.

If Christ came to church and sat in one of the pews, what then? Would not the minister constrain Him to preach to the people and allow himself to be a listener? If He were to decline and say: "I am among you as one that heareth," would he not beg Him at least to give the congregation some message of His own through the lips of the preacher? If an offering for the spread of the Gospel among the heathen were to be asked on that morning, would not the Master be besought to make the plea and to tell the people how He Himself "though rich, for our sakes became poor that we through his poverty might be rich"? If any strife existed in the flock, would there not be an earnest appeal to Him, the Good Shepherd, to guide His own sheep into the right way and to preserve the fold in peace?

Ah, yes. And Christ did come to church and abode there, but we knew it not, and therefore we took all the burden of teaching and collecting and governing on ourselves until we were often wearied with a load too heavy for us to bear. Well do we remember those days when drudgery was pushed to the point of desperation. The hearers must be moved to repentance and confession of Christ; therefore more effort must be devoted to the sermon, more hours to elaborating its periods, more pungency put into its sentences, more study bestowed on its delivery. And then came the disappointment that few, if any, were converted by all this which had cost a week of solid toil. And now attention was turned to the prayer meeting as the possible seat of the difficulty—so few attending it and so little readiness to participate in its services. A pulpit scourging must be laid on next Sunday, and the sharpest sting which words can effect put into the lash. Alas, there is no increase in the attendance, and instead of spontaneity in prayer and witnessing there is a silence which seems almost like sullenness! Then the administration goes wrong and opposition is encountered among officials, so that caucusing must be undertaken to get the members to vote as they should. Thus the burdens of anxiety increase while we are trying to lighten them, and should-be helpers become hinderers, until discouragement comes and sleepless nights ensue; these hot boxes on the train of our activities necessitating a stop and a visit of the doctor, with the verdict overwork and the remedy absolute rest.

It was after much of all this of which even the most

intimate friends knew nothing that there came one day a still voice of admonition, saying, *"There standeth one among you whom ye know not."* And perhaps I answered, "Who is he, Lord, that I might know him?" I had known the Holy Spirit as a heavenly influence to be invoked, but, somehow, I had not grasped the truth that He is a Person of the Godhead who came down to earth at a definite time and who has been in the church ever since, just as really as Jesus was here during the thirty and three years of His earthly life.

Precisely here was the defect. For it may be a question whose loss is the greater, his who thinks that Christ is present with him when He is not, or his who thinks not that Christ is present with him when He is. Recall the story of the missing child Jesus and how it is said that "they supposing him to be in the company went forward a day's journey." Alas, of how many nominal Christians is this true today! They journey on for years, saying prayers, reciting creeds, pronouncing confessions, giving alms, and doing duties, imagining all the time that because of these things Christ is with them. Happy are they if their mistake is not discovered too late for them to retrace their steps and to find through personal regeneration, the renewed heart which constitutes the absolute essential to companionship with the Son of God.

On the other hand, how many true Christians toil on, bearing burdens and assuming responsibilities far too great for their natural strength, utterly forgetful that the mighty Burden-bearer of the world is with them to do for them and through them that which they have undertaken to accomplish alone! Happy also for these if some weary day the blessed Paraclete, the invisible Christ, shall say to them, *"Have I been so long time with you and yet hast thou not known me?"* So it happened to the writer. The strong Son of God revealed Himself as being evermore in His church, and I knew Him, not through a sudden burst of revelation, not through some thrilling experience of instantaneous sanctification, but by a quiet, sure, and steady discovery, increasing to more and more. Jesus in the Spirit stood with me in a kind of spiritual epiphany and just as definitely and irrevocably as I once took Christ crucified as my sin-bearer I now took the Holy Spirit for my burden-bearer.

"Then you received the baptism of the Holy Spirit did you?" someone will ask. Well, we prefer not to use an expression which is not strictly biblical. The great promise, "Ye shall be baptized in the Holy Ghost," was fulfilled on the day of Pentecost once for all, as it seems to us. Then the Paraclete was given for the entire dispensation, and the whole church present and future was brought into the economy of the Spirit, as it is written: "For in one Spirit were we all baptized into one body" (1 Cor. 12:13, RV). But for God to give is one thing; for us to receive is quite another. "God so loved . . . that he gave his only begotten Son," is the word of our Lord to Nicodemus. But it is written also: "As many as *received* him to them gave he power to become the sons of God." In order to regeneration and sonship it is as absolutely essential for us to receive as for God to have given. So on the day of Pentecost the Holy Spirit, as the Comforter, Advocate, Helper, Teacher, and Guide, was given to the church. The disciples who before had been regenerated by the Spirit, as is commonly held, now received the Holy Spirit to qualify and empower them for service. It was another and higher experience than that which they had hitherto known. It is the difference between the Holy Spirit for renewal and the Holy Spirit for ministry. Even Jesus, begotten by the Holy Spirit and therefore called "the Son of God," did not enter upon His public service until He had been "anointed," or "sealed," with that same Spirit through whom He had been begotten. So of His immediate apostles; so of Paul, who had been converted on the way to Damascus. So of the others mentioned in the Acts, as the Samaritan Christians and the Ephesian disciples (Acts 19:1–8). And not a few thoughtful students of Scripture maintain that the same order still holds good, that there is such a thing as receiving the Holy Spirit in order to qualify for service. It is not denied that many may have this blessing in immediate connection with their conversion, from which it need not necessarily be separated. Only let it be marked that as the giving of the Spirit by the Father is plainly spoken of, so distinctly is the receiving of the Spirit on the part of the disciples constantly named in Scripture. When the risen Christ breathed on His disciples and said: "Receive ye the Holy Ghost," it is an active not a passive reception which is pointed out, as in the invitation: "Whosoever will, let him take the water of life freely." Here the same word is used as also in the Epistle to the Galatians. "Received ye the Spirit by the works of the law, or by the hearing of faith?" (Gal. 3:2).

God forbid that we should lay claim to any higher attainment than the humblest. We are simply trying to answer, as best we may from Scripture, the question asked above about the baptism of the Holy Spirit. On the whole, and after prolonged study of the Scripture, we cannot resist this conviction: As Christ, the second person of the Godhead, came to earth to make atonement for sin and to give eternal life, and as sinners we must receive Him by faith in order to obtain forgiveness and sonship, so the Holy Spirit, the third person of the Godhead, came to the earth to communicate the "power from on high"; and we must as believers in like manner receive Him by faith in order to be qualified for service. Both gifts have been bestowed, but it is not what we have but what we know that we have by a conscious appropriating faith which determines our spiritual wealth. Why, then, should we be satisfied with "the forgiveness of sins, according to the riches of his grace" (Eph. 1:7), when the Lord would grant us also "according to the riches of his glory, to be strengthened with might by his Spirit in the inner man"? (Eph. 3:16).

To return to personal experience, I am glad that one of the most conservative as well as eminent theological professors of our times has put this matter exactly as I should desire to see it stated. He says: "If a reference to personal experience may be permitted, I may indeed here set my seal. Never shall I forget the gain to conscious faith and peace which came to my own soul not long after the first decisive and appropriating view of the crucified Lord as the sinner's sacrifice of peace, from a more intelligent and conscious hold upon the living and most gracious personality of the Holy Spirit through whose mercy the soul had got that view. It was a new development of insight into the love of God. It was a new contact, as it were, with the inner and eternal movements of redeeming love and power, and a new discovery in divine resources. At such a time of finding gratitude and love and adoration we gain a new, a newly realized reason and motive power and rest."

"A conscious hold upon the personality of the Holy Spirit:" "a newly realized motive power." Such it was, not the sending down of some new power from heaven in answer to long waiting and prayer, but an "articulating into" a power already here, but hitherto imperfectly known and appropriated. Just in front of the study window where I write is a street above which it is said that a powerful electric current is constantly moving. I cannot see that current: it does not report itself to hearing, or sight, or taste, or smell, and so far as the testimony of the senses is to be taken, I might reasonably discredit its existence. But I see a slender arm, called the trolley, reaching up and touching it, and immediately the car with its heavy load of passengers moves along the track as though seized in the grasp of some mighty giant. The power had been there before, only now the car lays hold of it or is rather laid hold of by it, since it was a touch, not a grip, through which the motion was communicated. And would it be presumptuous for one to say that he had known something of a similar contact with not merely a divine force but a divine person? The change which ensued may be described thus: Instead of praying constantly for the descent of a divine influence there was now a surrender, however imperfect, to a divine and ever-present Being; instead of a constant effort to make use of the Holy Spirit for doing my work there arose a clear and abiding conviction that the true secret of service lay in so yielding to the Holy Spirit that He might use me to do His work. Would that the ideal might be so perfectly realized that over whatever remains of an earthly ministry, be it shorter or longer, might be written the slightly changed motto of Adolphe Monod:

> All through Christ: in the Holy spirit:
> for the glory of God. All else is nothing.

The Infilling of the Holy Spirit

Frederick Brotherton Meyer (1847–1929) was a "proper
Baptist pastor" until his life was transformed by working
with D. L. Moody in York in 1872. He pastored several
churches in England and founded Melbourne Hall,
Leicester, after the leadership at Victoria Road Baptist
Church opposed his evangelistic endeavors. He carried on
a popular itinerant ministry, and his emphasis on "the
deeper Christian life" brought new power and victory to
many defeated Christians. Spurgeon said, "Meyer preaches
as a man who has seen God face to face." He published
nearly one hundred books and booklets, among them a
series of biographies of great biblical characters.

This message is the ninth in a series Meyer gave in
Carnegie Hall, New York City, during an American tour.
It is taken from *A Castaway and Other Addresses*,
published in 1897 by Fleming H. Revell.

Frederick Brotherton Meyer

12

THE INFILLING OF THE HOLY SPIRIT

WE HAVE FOLLOWED Christ in His ascension, as entering the presence of His Father. He asked and received from God the Holy Spirit. We have also seen how Christ made Christians. "Christ" means "anointed"; " Christian" means "anointed one." The words "chrism" and "Christ" are identical in derivation. A man becomes truly a Christian when he is anointed with the Holy Spirit.

I speak now of the other aspect of Pentecost, because, though it is quite true that Pentecost means *the anointing on the head and heart*, it also means *the infilling of the Holy Spirit*. Therefore, in Acts 2:4 we are told that they were all—women and men, laymen and apostles— all were alike "filled with" the Holy Spirit.

Now, Ephesians 5:18 gives each one of us a positive command: "Be filled with the Spirit." It is very remarkable that in Acts 2 and Ephesians 5 the infilling of the Holy Spirit in its effect is compared to the effects of wine on the physical system. "Be not drunk with wine, wherein is excess, but be filled with the Spirit," and you can never have excess, you can never have too much of the Spirit.

There are three points of comparison that I want you to notice—joy, speech, power.

First. Wine produces a sense of exhilaration. A drunken man will sing as he reel's to his home; when a man is really filled with the Holy Spirit he becomes a singing Christian, and a Spirit-filled church is always a singing church. Every great outburst of the Holy Spirit's power has been accompanied by singing. Luther's revival spread through Germany by singing Luther's hymns. Whitfield was accompanied by a Wesley, and Moody by a Sankey, and in Germany the Moravian Church has given to us the songs of Gerhardt, with many more.

Secondly. A man who is filled with wine is garrulous. He talks; you cannot keep him still. And a man who is filled with the Holy Spirit talks, he cannot keep silence, he must tell what God has done.

Thirdly. A man who is filled with wine is conscious of a great increase of power. He feels as if he could stand alone against the world. So the man who is filled with the Holy Spirit is full also of the power of God.

Now this filling of the Holy Spirit may come suddenly, or more unconsciously, just as in Scotland they have what they call a "spate" of water, or a well may fill up with water percolating in drop by drop. Whenever the spirit of man, smitten with thirst, comes to Christ, and opens its whole content toward Christ, instantly Christ begins to infill that spirit. It may not be conscious of the gradual infilling, but by His grace He will never stay His hand until the earthly system has been filled to the very full from the river of God, which is full of water.

Now, there are three tenses used in the Greek of this filling. In Acts 13:52 we are told of the converts in the highlands of Galatia that they *were being filled* with joy and with the Holy Spirit all the time. They were like some mountain tarn which is always being filled from the melting of the snows above; and as the water flows on to enrich the pasture land beneath, so water is ever percolating in from the upper snow. O child of God, be a brimming lakelet or tarn, on the one hand always giving out to a dying world, but always kept full because you receive every moment from Jesus!

Then Acts 6:5 tells us that Stephen was a man *full of the Holy Spirit*—"full," the adjective; from which I gather that he was an equable man. He did not have fits and starts, he was not now lifted up and then depressed; but always, whenever you met Stephen, there was the same heavenly look, the same tender gracious word, the same perfect beauty of character, and the same eagerness to glorify Christ. O, beloved friends, I wish that you may keep on being filled, and that you may always be full!

And then, Acts 4:8 tells us that Peter, though he had

been filled on the day of Pentecost, nevertheless was suddenly *filled again* as he had to speak to the Sanhedrin. I suppose that for a moment he centered himself on God; he looked up, and received a sudden and immediate and complete equipment for his work.

Beloved minister, you may be a man full of the Holy Spirit in your family, but when you kneel in your vestry before entering your pulpit, before attempting a mission, before undertaking any definite work for God by lip or pen, be sure that you are specially equipped by a new reception of the Holy Spirit. In my own life I have found it absolutely necessary, after such a mission as this, when the whole system has become exhausted by the demand made upon the spirit, the nerve, and the physical strength, to get quietly away with God, and to renew one's strength by receiving out of the fullness of the Holy Spirit, breathing in a new supply.

Certain Definite Results

Now you will notice also that the work of the Holy Spirit of Pentecost, filling the heart, has in the character of the believer; and these are set forth by Christ in three verses, each of which begins with the words: "In that day." When the day of Pentecost breaks upon the spirit, it brings with it three distinct things.

In John 14:20 the Lord says: "*In that day*, in that day when the light of Pentecost has stolen through the window-pane of your heart, and has chased out the darkness, and has filled you within—in that day you shall know three things: (1) That I am in My Father, in the light of light, in the rare atmosphere of deity, in God. You shall know that I am in the Father, so that you will never be frightened of the Father again, but will come to Him at any moment knowing that I am in the heart of God. O child, you shall not fear God any more when the Holy Spirit has shown Jesus in Him. (2) That you are in Me. That is your standing. Your nature may be frail and fickle, your sins may sometimes overwhelm, but you shall know that I am in the Father, and you in me, accepted in the Beloved.

So near, so very near to God,
I cannot nearer be,
For in the person of His Son
I am as near as He.

(3) I in you. That is what I spoke of in a preceding address, the revelation of the indwelling Christ.

It is a beautiful thing to know that the 14th chapter of John begins with our mansion or abiding place (R.V. Marg.) with God and ends with God's mansion or abiding-place with us; for the same word which is used of the mansions of the Father's house in the second verse is used in the twenty-third verse of God's mansion in the spirit of the believer.

Men say to me: "Is not this mysticism that you teach?"

I answer: "Every mystic is not a Christian, but every Christian is bound to be a mystic, because mysticism is the indwelling of God."

Religion among the Hindus is the indwelling of God, but it disappoints them; they cannot reach it because they seek it by endeavoring for the absorption of themselves, the loss of their individuality, in God. We as Christians seek also to know the indwelling of God, but it is not by the loss of our individuality, but by the reception of God's nature as the determining power working through the individuality which He has given to us. "Ye shall know that I am in the Father, and ye in me, and I in you."

Now turn to John 16:23: "And *in that day* ye shall ask me nothing." The Greek word is: "Ye shall ask me no questions."

Up to that time the disciples kept asking questions suggested by the intellect, curious questions; but when the day of Pentecost came they did not need to ask questions with the intellect because they saw truth with the heart.

If I am blind, I ask my friend concerning the landscape: "Are there mountains?" "Yes." "Rivers?" "Yes." "Cornfields?" "Yes." I ask question after question, and get what help I can. But when my eyes are opened, or when the light of the morning breaks, I ask no more questions about the contour, the configuration of the landscape, because I see it for myself.

Before you have the power of the Holy Spirit you will be curious about many questions; but when the Holy Spirit shall come you shall know all things clearly with the heart. I often think that woman's nature enables me to understand how we know in the power of the Holy Spirit. A man is said to reason his way, a woman by the quick glance of her intuition sees what she cannot reason, and she jumps to a conclusion to which her husband reasons his way ten minutes later. So is it with the heart when it is illumined by the Holy Spirit. The pure heart of the believer leaps to conclusions which eye has not seen, nor ear heard, nor the reason of man conceived. The faculty of knowledge is altered: we no longer seek it by the intellect, but by the heart. The busy intellectual disputant becomes the deep intuitioner.

And then, thirdly, turn to John 16:26; "*In that day* ye shall ask in my name."

Now in the Bible "name" stands for "nature," and you are always perfectly justified in substituting the word "nature" for "name." So Christ says that when the day of Pentecost has come, we shall ask in His nature, or rather, that His nature will ask through us; whenever the nature of Jesus asks anything of the Father, it asks that which the Father is bound to give, because He and Jesus are one.

In one's earlier life one asks for a great many things which God never gives; and we are sometimes startled, and begin to think that prayer is inoperative. But further on in life we allow our prayers to pass the test of the nature of Christ; as one request after another arises in our hearts, we bring it into the light of the nature of Jesus, and there are a great many things that we therefore reject. I cannot ask this, I dare not ask that, I feel that they would be incongruous with the nature of my Lord, which now has become my nature, and so would ask only in the nature of Christ.

I find in my own life that I do not pray quite so long as I used. I pray more slowly. I sit, or stand, or wait before

God until I tell what Christ is wanting at that moment, and when in my heart, by the Holy Spirit, the prayer of my Lord is made clear to me, I take it up. I launch my little canoe upon the current of my Savior's intercession, and I have what I ask.

There are indeed two Advocates, two Paracletes. There is the Paraclete in the heart of God—Jesus; and there is the Paraclete in the heart of the believer—the Holy Spirit; these two Paracletes are one. When the Holy Spirit breathes your prayer, He will inspire that which it is on the heart of Jesus to entreat, and you have the perfect circle of prayer—the Father, the Son, the Holy Spirit in you, your voice raised in unison with the music of the Holy Trinity; so the desire which emanated from God the Father, and was reflected in His nature by Christ the Son, and was communicated to you by the Holy Spirit, is flashed back from you, and you know you have the petitions that you desire of Him.

The Philosophy of Prayer

But there is a fourth work of the Spirit of God. In John 15:26–27, it is said: "He, (that is, the Spirit) shall *bear witness of Me*, and ye shall bear witness."

Now the church is in the world not to argue, not to defend God, not to stand forth as an advocate for God, but simply to witness to the truth of the unseen and eternal. And directly, brother ministers, you and I step away from that position, and become advocates pleading instead of witnesses bearing testimony, we step away from the position of power. You and I and the church are called to bear witness to the death of Christ, His resurrection, His ascension, and the advent of the Holy Spirit. You can talk as you like about His social work, about His teaching, about the philosophy of the administration of His kingdom; but your *prime* work is to stand up before men, and say:

"I have known and tasted and handled of the death, resurrection, ascension and return of Jesus Christ our Lord."

And while you do that the Holy Spirit says: "Amen."

The other day I came on a saw pit. I could see a man sawing a great beam of timber with the long saw which rose and fell, and though I could not see his confederate, I knew that down in the pit there was another man who had hold of the saw; and I could tell the rhythm and the motion of the body of the man I could not see, by noticing the rhythm and the motion of the body of the man I could see. And I saw at once that that was an illustration of the co-witness of the Holy Spirit.

When a man stands up in his pulpit and says; "Jesus died," the Holy Spirit says: "He did, and it was by Me that He offered Himself to God." When the minister says: "He rose," the Holy Spirit says: "He did: and it was by My power that He was raised and declared to be the Son of God." When we say: "He went back to God and liveth and reigneth with the Father," the Holy Spirit, brooding in the church, says: "Yea, Amen, I have just left Him; I am in loving fellowship with Him; I and the Son and the Father are one."

O, brother ministers, ever since I learned this, my work has been quite altered, because now, when I enter my pulpit, I go as only a very small part of the great machinery which is in operation. I have to speak, but the Holy Spirit is all the time working with me, and hence the salvation of my people does not stand in the wisdom of men, but in the power and demonstration of the Holy Spirit. If they received simply upon my putting of it, the effect would be evanescent, but when the Holy Spirit demonstrates a thing to the conscience it is permanent.

You and I were once at school. We had a problem in geometry. We might have seen at a glance that such and such a thing must be so, but we were called upon to demonstrate it, and the demonstration would be our conclusion. So the Holy Spirit establishes the word of the child, the servant of God, in the Bible class, in the mission, and in the church.

In London, in the winter, after the services of the church are over, we have our magic-lantern service from nine to ten o'clock for people whose clothes are too shabby to come among the more respectable audiences. It is so dark that Nicodemus does not mind coming in. I carefully prepare my sermon and keep one proof of it and give the other to my secretary, who operates from the gallery. I begin to preach. When I say: "God so loved the world that He gave His only begotten Son," I know that as I utter the words he flashes on the screen behind me a picture of the world, a globe with a scroll around it: "God is love." When I say: "Now is the time to accept this Christ," the word "now" will appear behind me. And if I speak of the Savior's dying love and pity, instantly I know, by previous agreement, that Doré's picture of the crucified Christ is appealing to the people. I do not need to look to see if it is there, because the awe, the reverence, the silence of the people indicate to me that that great sight is represented on the canvas. My secretary demonstrates to the eye what I say to the ear.

Partnership with the Holy Spirit

My meaning, I trust, is distinct. You and I may go to work for God—a "partnership with the Holy Spirit"—so to speak. The word "communion," which the minister invokes upon the people as they leave, means fellowship, common action; the minister stands before the people in the communion of the Holy Spirit, and the Holy Spirit demonstrates the word he feebly speaks.

O, men of God, mind that you are always so filled with the Spirit that wherever you go the Holy Spirit may be prepared to go with you. You know the old Welsh story of the crowded congregation that waited for John Ellis. They sent for him. The man came back to say: "I heard him talking to somebody, and I did not like to disturb him." They said: "Go again and rap." He went, and came back and said: "I heard him talking still, and I heard him say, 'I will not go unless you come along too.'" John Ellis came in five minutes later, and the One he had been talking to came with him, though no one saw Him; and they had a meeting of wonderful power. Brother ministers, never go unless He comes too.

In Acts 11:15, Peter, speaking about Cornelius and the descent of the Holy Spirit in Cornelius' house, says rather ruefully, as if he looked back on a sermon which was only half delivered:

"As I began to speak, the Holy Spirit fell."

Peter had only gotten through his introduction—he had not got as far as his first head—and the Holy Spirit came down, and said:

"Man, you have made a good start, and into your introduction you have put the life and death and work of Jesus. That is text enough for me. Now stand aside, and I will finish the sermon."

"As I began to speak!" Why, I am thankful to God if I have been able to speak for half an hour, and toward the end of my sermon I can see the Holy Spirit has fallen upon my people. But O that we might be so filled with the Spirit and care so much about the cooperation of the Spirit that it might be with us as with Finney or Peter. It is said of Finney, more than once in his autobiography, that if he came into a large factory or into a church crowded with people, there was such an indescribable power about his very aspect that in many cases a revival broke out before Finney could speak a word. Men, brother ministers, let us aim for that!

Now, finally, here are the seven conditions on which you may have this mighty cooperating power.

Seven Conditions

1. You must be *Holy Spirit filled.* Peter was filled thrice; once in the second chapter of Acts, and twice in the fourth chapter. He was a Holy Spirit filled man in character, and therefore he could count on the cooperation of the Spirit.

2. You must be *emptied.* Peter was empty. He spent many days in a tanner's house. I can hardly imagine how he got into such an emptying place. In the first place, it was a very insalubrious spot. Of all hotels it is about the last place I would select. The odor would be anything but savory. And then, in the next place, as a Jew it must have been defiling to him to be in such close association with carcasses. And yet he spent many days as in a city alley; this apostle, this man who had preached through large regions, who had raised Eneas and Dorcas, got down to the tanner's house. And a man will have to come to an end of himself before the Holy Spirit will work with him.

3. You must be *a man of prayer*. Peter was a man of prayer. Acts 10:9: "Peter went up upon the housetop to pray, about the sixth hour." Some may think that when I say: "Do not pray so much, but take," I mean that they are to give up their lonely hours of fellowship with God. Not at all. No true experience can ever exist apart from communion with God. But mind, instead of asking for so many things that God cannot give, you will ask for a few things definitely, you will be led out in prayer, you will feel you cannot help praying for those few things, and you will have so much to do in praising and thanking God for giving you your heart's desire that your prayer times will tend to be longer rather than shorter.

4. You must be *willing to give up prejudice*. When Peter was first commanded to kill and eat of the creatures let down from heaven in the sheet, he said: "Not so, Lord: for I have never eaten anything that is common or unclean." But after thinking about the vision, he was willing to give up lifelong prejudices.

I have met men in my life who have refused to receive these teachings about the Holy Spirit, which in these latter days God has made known to His church. They have said with Peter:

"Not so, Lord. I believe in the good old way of putting things, and I refuse to accept any further light that may break from Thy Word."

That very often stereotypes a man's power. He cannot advance with God. If Peter had refused to advance with God, God would have gone on without him. Be sure to advance with God.

5. You must be *Spirit-guided*. This also was true of Peter. The Spirit said: "Three men seek thee; go with them."

Now listen. Never take an impulse in your heart as being final. It may be of the Devil, or it may be of the Spirit of God. The Devil often comes as an angel of light, but you may always know when the impulse is of God, first, by its becoming a settled purpose. You may always know the Devil because he asks questions. The Devil always deals with notes of interrogation, and whenever you have a lot of notes of interrogation flitting about your mind, you know it is the dust raised by the Devil. When God deals with you He is always definite, and the impression grows stronger every time you pray. But any impression from God's Spirit is always corroborated by two things: by the Word, and by circumstances. The Spirit of God and the Word of God are parallel lines. And if you are truly called of God, circumstances will coincide with the spiritual impulse. The inward impulse, the Word of God, and the outward circumstance will be in line. So it was with Peter. The Spirit said: "Three men seek thee," and suddenly he heard three men rapping downstairs. Always wait for the knock of the man, as well as the impulse from the Holy Spirit, agreeing with the Word of God.

6. You must be *humble*. When this Roman officer fell before Peter the fisherman, Peter lifted him up, and said: "Stand on your feet; I also am a man." There was nothing of the priest about Peter. In our country the priest is rather glad to have a man at his feet; but Peter, a sincere transparent servant of God, did not look down, but said:

"Man, stand up!"

A truly humble soul is necessary for the cooperation of the Holy Spirit.

7. You must *seek the glory of Christ*.

My secretary and I agree upon our sermon for the magic lantern service before we start; and if you want the Holy Spirit to help you in your preaching, you and the Holy Spirit must agree together what you are going to preach about. If you are going to talk about social reform, I should not be at all surprised if the Holy Spirit should say:

"If you are going to preach that, you must do it yourself, for I will have nothing to do with it."

You will say: "I want to preach on the last political crisis."

The Holy Spirit will answer: "Very well, go on; but you must go your own way. I cannot help you with that."

Or you will come to the Holy Spirit, and say: "Blessed Spirit, what shall I preach from?" and there will steal into your heart the name "JESUS!" and the Holy Spirit will say:

"You may begin where you like, you may deal with any

historical subject you like, but you must end with the Lord Jesus Christ."

Some time ago one of my friends went out with a little boy who was leading him across the common from the railroad station to the house. My friend said to him;

"Go to Sunday school?"

"Yes."

"What did your teacher talk about last Sunday afternoon?"

"O, he was talking about Jacob."

"And what did he take the Sunday before that?"

"O, he was talking about prayer."

"Well, did your teacher talk about Jesus?"

"O, no," said the little fellow, "that's at the other end of the book."

Now I hold that Jesus is not at the other end of the Book, but He is all through the Book, and every chapter and every verse and every incident in the Bible may somehow be made a road to Jesus.

I do not say that on week evenings a minister may not deal with public questions. No doubt the world will stand still until he tells it what to do. But I do think that while he has a desire for the discussion of those great problems, with the reporters listening, whether on week evening or on Sunday, for the most part—I am not offering to lay down any absolute rule, because in the case of arbitration, when fear spread over our hearts that our two great sister countries might be embroiled in strife, the pulpit spoke out and saved (as I believe) the question from becoming serious on each side of the Atlantic—but for the most part there must be the constant uplifting of the Lord Jesus Christ in His glory as the Savior of men. And as you dare to do that simply and humbly, the power of God the Holy Spirit will witness to the living Christ in your church, in the Sunday school. It matters little enough to God what you are in intellectual power, or natural gifts and eloquence. He simply wants a nature yielded absolutely to Him, and a voice raised for Jesus, and the Holy Spirit will do everything else.